ROUTLEDGE LIBRARY EDITIONS:
LIBRARY AND INFORMATION SCIENCE

Volume 59

MONOGRAPHS IN SCI-TECH LIBRARIES

MONOGRAPHS IN SCI-TECH LIBRARIES

Edited by
ELLIS MOUNT

LONDON AND NEW YORK

First published in 1983 by The Haworth Press, Inc.

This edition first published in 2020
by Routledge
2 Park Square, Milton Park, Abingdon, Oxon OX14 4RN

and by Routledge
52 Vanderbilt Avenue, New York, NY 10017

Routledge is an imprint of the Taylor & Francis Group, an informa business

© 1983 The Haworth Press, Inc.

All rights reserved. No part of this book may be reprinted or reproduced or utilised in any form or by any electronic, mechanical, or other means, now known or hereafter invented, including photocopying and recording, or in any information storage or retrieval system, without permission in writing from the publishers.

Trademark notice: Product or corporate names may be trademarks or registered trademarks, and are used only for identification and explanation without intent to infringe.

British Library Cataloguing in Publication Data
A catalogue record for this book is available from the British Library

ISBN: 978-0-367-34616-4 (Set)
ISBN: 978-0-429-34352-0 (Set) (ebk)
ISBN: 978-0-367-36375-8 (Volume 59) (hbk)
ISBN: 978-0-367-36376-5 (Volume 59) (pbk)
ISBN: 978-0-429-34553-1 (Volume 59) (ebk)

Publisher's Note
The publisher has gone to great lengths to ensure the quality of this reprint but points out that some imperfections in the original copies may be apparent.

Disclaimer
The publisher has made every effort to trace copyright holders and would welcome correspondence from those they have been unable to trace.

Monographs in Sci-Tech Libraries

Ellis Mount, Editor

The Haworth Press
New York

Monographs in Sci-Tech Libraries has also been published as *Science & Technology Libraries,* volume 3, number 3, Spring 1983.

Copyright © 1983 by The Haworth Press, Inc. All rights reserved. Copies of articles in this work may be reproduced noncommercially for the purpose of educational or scientific advancement. Otherwise, no part of this work may be reproduced or utilized in any form or by any means, electronic or mechanical including photocopying, microfilm, and recording, or by any information storage and retrieval system, without permission in writing from the publisher. Printed in the United States of America.

The Haworth Press, Inc., 28 East 22 Street, New York, NY 10010

Library of Congress Cataloging in Publication Data
Main entry under title:

Monographs in sci-tech libraries.

    "Has also been published as Science & Technology libraries, volume 3, number 3, Spring 1983"—T.p. verso.
    Includes bibliographical references.
    1. Scientific libraries. 2. Technical libraries. 3. Collection development (Libraries) I. Mount, Ellis.
Z675.T3M685 1983   026'.5   82-23435
ISBN 0-86656-218-4

Monographs in Sci-Tech Libraries

Science & Technology Libraries
Volume 3, Number 3

CONTENTS

EDITORIAL	1

Monographic Works in Sci-Tech Libraries
    Stuart J. Glogoff
    Martha J. Bailey
	3

Collection Development in Science and Technology: A Focus on Books *Marianne Cooper*	15

The Acquisition of Monographs in Large Academic Scientific Research Libraries: Current Issues and Problems
    Maxine H. Reneker
    Suzanne Fedunok
	31

Sources of Information Used by Selectors in Four Medical School Libraries for Collection Development *Beatrice Kovacs*	53
A Brief Study of Unaffiliated Research Level Monograph Authors *Robert G. Krupp*	65
The Monograph is Not Endangered—But Its Package is Changing *Gary Craig*	69

NEW REFERENCE WORKS IN SCIENCE AND TECHNOLOGY *Janice W. Bain, Editor*	77
SCI-TECH ONLINE *Ellen Nagle, Editor*	85
SCI-TECH IN REVIEW *Suzanne Fedunok, Editor*	93
LETTER TO THE EDITOR	101

EDITORIAL

The monograph as a distinctive type of literature has had a long and distinguished history, dating back to the appearance of the first treatises on scientific subjects in the late fifteenth century. In the period since then monographs have played a significant role in all types of sci-tech libraries.

This issue is devoted to a consideration of the present contributions monographs are making in such libraries as well as their probable role in the future. Several related topics are also included, such as sources for obtaining monographs, tools used for selecting them and the attitude of publishers towards their creation.

In the first paper Stuart J. Glogoff and Martha J. Bailey present a review of the various formats in which monographs appear, along with comments on the features of each variant. The next paper, by Marianne Cooper, discusses the sources used to obtain information about monographic works, as well as principles of collection development.

The problems of large academic libraries in the budgeting, selection and preservation of scientific/technical monographs are reviewed in the paper by Maxine H. Reneker and Suzanne Fedunok. Beatrice Kovacs reports on a survey of four medical school libraries in regard to the tools they use in making selections for their collections.

A topic not often discussed in the literature—the question of how many sci-tech monographs include information on the professional affiliation of their authors—is the subject of a brief study made by Robert G. Krupp. The last paper is by Gary Craig, who presents the viewpoint of a major sci-tech publisher in regard to the future of monographs, including predictions of the types of formats they may have in the years ahead.

The issue is rounded out with our regular sections.

Ellis Mount

Monographic Works in Sci-Tech Libraries

Stuart J. Glogoff
Martha J. Bailey

ABSTRACT. This paper reviews the nature and types of monographs used in science and technology libraries. The types of monographic works discussed are: books and textbooks, handbooks, encyclopedias and dictionaries, government documents and technical reports, patents, patent reviews and tabular compilations, laboratory notebooks, progress reports, dissertations, manufacturers' catalogs and directories of manufacturers, and new serial directories. Following this discussion, several guides listing specific monographs are recommended.

INTRODUCTION

Science and technology libraries serve as repositories for a variety of primary and secondary source materials that appear in monographic form. These materials may include raw data recorded in lab notebooks, statistical or tabular data compiled in handbooks, and articles or book chapters reviewing the state-of-the-art of a subject in a specialized field. Obviously, librarians and information specialists in sci-tech libraries must be able to work effectively amid the gamut of scientific monographs. This paper outlines the various types of scientific monographs and discusses relevant strengths and weaknesses in an effort to provide a background article for the beginning librarian and practitioner.

BOOKS AND TEXTBOOKS

Books and textbooks on scientific subjects can make important contributions by synthesizing the state of knowledge on a topic at a certain point. Most often such books are devoted to narrow subject

---

Stuart Glogoff is Associate Librarian and Head, Circulation Department, University of Delaware Library, Newark, DE 19711. He holds the MLS degree from Indiana University. Martha J. Bailey is Professor of Library Sciences and Life Sciences Librarian, Purdue University, West Lafayette, IN 47907. She received the MLS degree from Drexel University.

© 1983 by The Haworth Press, Inc. All rights reserved.

areas and are written because of a distinctly perceived need. Two recently published monographs serve as examples. The first, *Sediment Microbiology,* provides students and practitioners in this specialized field with a book covering what the authors declare is "a neglected area of aquatic microbiology."[1] In the preface to the second work, *Astronomical Photometry,* the reason given for writing the book is that "books for newcomers to this field are almost totally lacking."[2] Information in the book focuses upon observation techniques, construction, and reference materials. Both are well illustrated with photographs, tables, formulas, and drawings.

Textbooks in the sciences can represent an extensive literature review on a subject and contain many useful references to previous research making them a valuable tool for college courses. Unfortunately, as every college student knows, textbooks are often expensive and become outdated with new developments in the field. Academic and research libraries are reluctant to acquire textbooks for these reasons and regularly exclude them from profiles in approval plans. Standard textbooks must undergo frequent revisions to ensure current applicability. Any textbook, therefore, must be carefully evaluated.

While books and textbooks are valuable sources for summarizing the state of knowledge at one stage, they are not a sufficient means to communicate research findings. Scientists and engineers will not devote their time to writing textbooks or monographs on a topic that all too quickly becomes outdated. An example of the problem of writing a monograph in an area where information changes rapidly occurred in the medical specialty ultrasound, where the technology in this field changed fundamentally three times in two years. One book failed in the market by being four months out-of-date when published.[3]

Furthermore, the main reason books are not a critical means of advancing scientific knowledge is seen in the time devoted to their preparation. To begin with, researching a topic broad enough to produce sufficient material for a book takes many months, if not years. In the physical sciences, a study observed that the average time between when an author initiated work on a project until it appeared as an article was 26 months.[4] Lab and clinical research papers in the medical sciences averaged four years from idea to publication, according to an analysis of 103 papers by Mayo Clinic authors.[5] Added to the necessary research time, is the time spent writing, editing, publishing, and marketing the book. Unlike journals, where subscriptions virtually guarantee an audience, books are largely sold on a one-by-one basis through mass mailings to potential readers, because of advertisements or a review in a journal catching a reader's attention, by word of mouth, and library approval plans. Certainly, the scope of the work and the necessity for timeliness may often work against book and textbook publishing in the sciences.

HANDBOOKS

Handbooks organize a vast amount of data in a convenient form. Most often, handbooks are concise compilations of data on a specific topic, such as the *Handbook of Mathematical Formulas* or the *Handbook of Laboratory Animal Science*. Generally, scientific handbooks collect a large body of technical information called "established knowledge" that does not change. This includes basic data and formulas. New editions of these types of handbooks are rare, usually prepared every 10 to 20 years. For fields where information changes more regularly, such as the engineering sciences, volumes must be revised within 5 years. This is especially true in the materials sciences where there are rapid advances in developing new electronics materials. Sometimes, sources updating the data in handbooks will be published by manufacturers as bulletins or brochures. The *ASTM Book of Standards,* a basic set that is issued annually, illustrates this.

Some researchers feel more comfortable using an older edition of a handbook than a more recent, revised edition. After years of faithful service it is like an old and trusted friend. Unfortunately, in some fields this can be disastrous. The composition and characteristics of metals and other materials, for example, undergo constant revisions that can affect the success of a design or experiment. Safety standards, such as those for handling toxic and formerly non-toxic materials, face rapid revision under the Occupational Safety and Health Administration's review. Failing to use the most up-to-date handbook on laboratory safety could easily prove hazardous to one's health.

SPECIALIZED ENCYCLOPEDIAS AND DICTIONARIES

Because scientists depend on the journal literature to satisfy their information needs and with an increasing interest in the work done in allied fields, it is not unusual to encounter unfamiliar terms, concepts, or processes. For this reason, an encyclopedia offering informative articles on technical subjects is needed to enable the researcher to become familiar with unfamiliar subjects. In addition, librarians and information specialists are making more use of subject encyclopedias to prepare better search strategies for online bibliographic data base searching.

Specialized encyclopedias may be single volume works or multi-volume sets. They may concentrate on a particular science, like the one-volume *McGraw-Hill Encyclopedia of Environmental Science* or be broadly based like *Van Nostrand's Scientific Encyclopedia* to cover virtually all scientific fields. The premiere all-purpose multi-volume scientific encyclopedia is the *McGraw-Hill Encyclopedia of Science and Technology,* in its 5th edition at the time of this writing. This 15-volume set is the standard from which subject encyclopedias may be measured. Several thousand contributors have written tens of thousands of articles. Longer discussions are well-illustrated with technical charts, tables, maps, and diagrams. The name of the article's author is given, as are references to recommended additional readings. Volume 15, the index, offers access to information through a topical index and an analytical index to textual material as well as to information in illustrations, legends, tables, and maps.

Scientific dictionaries can best be divided into two general categories: English language and foreign language. English language scientific dictionaries often provide short discussions of terms which are especially important for terms with different meanings in different fields. In the *McGraw-Hill Dictionary of Scientific and Technical Terms,* 2nd edition, "web" has multiple definitions reflecting its different meanings in architecture, civil engineering, graphics, materials, mechanical engineering, meteorology, optics, textiles, and vertebrate zoology. Foreign language scientific dictionaries may be bilingual or multilingual. In most cases the English term is given with its foreign equivalent in the next column. Rarely in a sci-tech multilingual dictionary is a word's meaning given.

Considering how specialized is the terminology of technology and how, in today's society, terminology changes so rapidly, the need for precise scientific and technological dictionaries is great. Librarians and information specialists must consider these sources as an integral part of the reference collection. Selecting one or two that are deemed most reliable will come from their frequent use.

GOVERNMENT DOCUMENTS AND TECHNICAL REPORTS

The U.S. government, acknowledged as the largest publisher in the world, generates a variety of primary source materials. Hundreds of offices within the government are involved daily in research and development (R&D), whether conducting the research at a government facility or farming it out to industrial and academic researchers. Some government documents are only a few pages long and cover general interest topics such as reading food labels, selecting day-care facilities or dealing with alcoholism. Those that most researchers in scientific fields use are the detailed, technical reports of R&D projects.

These technical reports give the progress or results of research and development investigations. Although the technical report has existed for more than 100 years, its importance to communicating scientific information increased dramatically after World War II. The U.S. government precipitated much of this by compiling and publishing reports describing German technical data. As federal funding for industrial and academic research mushroomed over the next two decades, the technical report became the standard format for disseminating R&D results.

Initially, a researcher or company submits a technical report to the project's funding agency. Then the funding agency distributes copies to companies and individuals designated as having a "need to know" of the project's fundings. A company may then list the availability of its technical reports in an announcements bulletin. Scientists interested in reading a copy can usually order one at a nominal cost.

Government funding agencies publish sources listing their outside contracts. Depending on the field of research, a scientist will closely follow what projects a particular agency is funding. This, of course, is important in applying for a grant as well as keeping informed of relevant reports. The National Aeronautics and Space Administration, for example, publishes a restricted and non-restricted edition of its *Scientific and Technical Aerospace Reports (STAR)*. The Department of Defense, similarly, publishes a *Technical Abstracts Bulletin (TAB)* and the U.S. Energy Research and Development Administration lists contract reports in its *Energy Research Abstracts*.

Fortunately, there is a source linking the various agencies and centralizing access to their available technical reports. The National

Technical Information Service (NTIS) acts as a clearinghouse for all unclassified federally sponsored research and development reports. These reports are listed in the *Government Reports Announcements and Index,* published since 1946 under varying titles. It provides such vital information as the authors, title, contract number, sponsoring agency, contractor, report number and the order number of the technical report. An abstract is also furnished.

Other government documents may be listed in the *Monthly Catalog of U.S. Government Publications,* published since 1895, and available from the Superintendent of Documents. In addition, thousands of documents are available to the public throughout the country in designated government document depository libraries. These libraries are usually part of a federal, university, large public, or state library. Considering the volume of sci-tech reports published by the government and their multifarious method of distribution, scientists and engineers must often consult a librarian or information specialist to locate needed documents. Currently, there are scores of sources to government documents and some that are currently available through database searching services.

PATENTS

Patents always have been a major source of information for researchers in chemical, pharmaceutical, and electronics research. Recent changes in the interpretation of the patent laws now permit inventors or patentees to patent such diverse forms as living organisms or computer software. For this reason, it is necessary to understand the types of information contained in patents. Librarians and information scientists with accurate information of existing and pending patents may save researchers the agony of duplicating another scientist's work and reduce the possibilities of litigation from infringing upon a patent belonging to another party.

A common practice before a project is undertaken in an industrial research setting is for the library staff to conduct a literature search and for the patent attorneys to do a quick patent search. Many companies, for good reason, will not allocate funds for a project until these two preliminary steps have taken place. Consider the consequences of the independent researcher who is forced to pay for patent infringements. The fees easily could result in bankruptcy. In industry, a researcher can face dismissal for undertaking a project without permission. Involving the company in a law suit can ruin a career.

Patents consist of a legal statement of the claim with such supporting evidence as diagrams, formulas, or citations. The document mentions the inventor and patentee, who are not necessarily the same. Persons working in industrial research normally sign a patent release with their employer. Any ideas they develop belong to the employer contingent upon payment of an agreed fee. The amount may be as little as $1.00 or it may be a negotiated percentage of the profits. Since patents are honored only in the countries issuing them, the same patent normally is filed and issued in several countries. An American patent might also be filed in such countries as Great Britain, France, Germany, and Japan.

The U.S. Patent Office Search Center in Arlington, Virginia, maintains a complete file of patents and their records. Anyone may order copies of original patents or consult them at a regional patent copy depository library. Patent attorneys and agents often obtain the supporting records for patents to aid in preparing their patent applications, paying only a fair charge for the photocopying.

In a corporation, patent attorneys or agents review scientists' internal proprietary reports to determine what ideas may be patentable. The attorneys prepare the proper documents and file a patent application with the U.S. Patent Office. The supporting records often consist of data from laboratory notebooks and proprietary reports. Since the application is a public record, people with a need to know may examine the applications and supporting records, although the patent itself may not be granted for several years.

PATENT REVIEWS AND TABULAR COMPILATIONS

Although the patent literature is a rather specialized field, many journals include information on current patents and trademarks. Several journals, in fact, exclusively feature this literature. Four representative titles are the *Trademark Review, International Licensing* (which has the explanatory subtitle "Monthly bulletin providing an international forum for the negotiation of manufacturing licenses and joint ventures"), and the two Derwent Services reviews, *U.S. Patents Report* and *World Patents Abstracts Journal.* Other journals, like the *Journal of Applied Chemistry, Applied Optics, IBM Journal of Research and Development, RCA Review,* and *Solid State Technology,* publish news or abstracts about new patents.

Many scientific journals publish papers consisting of tabular information that is later compiled in handbooks of tables. The American Chemical Society, American Institute of Physics, and National Bureau of Standards have joined in publishing a journal for such data entitled the *Journal of Physical and Chemical Reference Data.* The *Journal of Research* of the National Bureau of Standards also contains selected papers on these types of data. In addition there are government agencies which fund data centers throughout the country that gather and disseminate information about selected materials and properties. An example is the Center for Information and Numerical Data Analysis and Synthesis (CINDAS) at Purdue University. CINDAS issues a newsletter for its Electronic Properties Information Center and Thermophysical Properties Research Center that reports research data. The data later are included in the Center's commercially published handbooks.

LABORATORY NOTEBOOKS

One vehicle widely used by scientists in industrial and academic settings as a daily log of ideas, thoughts, summaries and data is the laboratory notebook. Lab notebooks represent a compendium of all the essential facts and details of a research project. Separate notebooks are maintained for each project and may be numbered or indexed by staff librarians or information specialists and issued to other scientists and technicians. Special conditions, such as those imposed on projects carrying a security classification or by patent attorneys, affect the procedures for issuing, processing, and storing laboratory notebooks.

While library-information service personnel in industrial settings often become involved in processing lab notebooks, this is not the case in academic institutions. Instead, the scientist or department has retained control of the laboratory notebook. Recent changes in patent laws, however, may cause universities to review these procedures. While the new laws facilitate applying for patents, universities may face instituting more control over lab notebooks to assure that all the data necessary to support a patent claim is available. For scientists in academic institutions, developments in this area will be followed with great interest.

PROGRESS REPORTS

Progress reports can take several forms, usually depending on whether the report is prepared for an external or internal audience. For example, government contracts require submitting quarterly or interim progress reports to the funding agency as standard procedure. These reports are summarized in an annual report or a formal summary report on the contract. Within the company, a controlled distribution list is used to circulate monthly progress reports, departmental reports and memoranda. These reports contain proprietary data often unavailable in other sources. Many companies selectively condense information from their progress reports to feature in instruction manuals, catalogs, circulars, and brochures prepared for clients and prospective customers. All of these publications also contain information about processes and products that may not be otherwise available. Finally, company newsletters and magazines often report unique information submitted by researchers. Many companies find it beneficial to utilize the writing skills of technical editors to prepare material destined for circulation outside the company.

DISSERTATIONS

The dissertation, the vehicle for disseminating a doctoral candidate's research results, is one of the least appreciated and least used sources of scientific information. A study of doctoral dissertation use[6] concentrating on the fields of chemistry, chemical engineering, botany, and psychology revealed that 53% of the dissertations studied had not been cited in the published literature. In addition, it was found that the argument that dissertation information at least results in a journal article was exaggerated. Twenty-three percent of the chemistry dissertations and 57% of those in psychology failed to yield a publication. Those that do appear in the journal literature probably report less data than is presented in the dissertion.

Besides these problems, there are also difficulties with their physical access. Libraries, as a rule, do not acquire them unless specifically requested to by researchers or scholars. Furthermore, few libraries will loan a dissertation. People who want to read one are forced to order a microfilm copy or a photocopied reproduction from University Microfilms International, the company publishing *Dissertation Abstracts International.* Their 1982 charges in the U.S. and Canada are $12.00 for microfilm copy and $22.00 for a photocopy. Shipping and handling charges are extra. The total cost for obtaining one dissertation may be high enough to discourage a number of potential users from placing orders.

There are a few institutions that neither deposit their dissertations in *Dissertations Abstracts International* nor lend them to requesting libraries. Harvard, where valuable research findings are reported in dissertations each year, has such a policy. In Harvard's case, it also charges exorbitant fees for photocopied theses and dissertations. Certainly, such practices make it more difficult when a major research institution fails to make its sources readily available. Understandably, some people do not try to acquire them since it seems like so much bother. Considering the time, effort, and value of original scientific research, it is unfortunate that dissertations are not more readily available.

MANUFACTURERS' CATALOGS AND DIRECTORIES OF MANUFACTURERS

Trade literature in the form of manufacturers' catalogs often is the only source for information about products and specifications. When a company is the only producer for a computer chip or a type of steel tubing, the catalogs represent the only source for information on the products. The material takes many forms: bound catalogs, price sheets, specification sheets, diagrams, engineering drawings, brochures, and wiring diagrams. There is no single source for learning about products. Most of the trade journals include postal cards on which readers can request information on the products which are advertised. Although many large purchasing departments index their files of trade catalogs, most companies and organizations have files and stacks of this type of material scattered throughout offices and work areas.

There are several compilations of this type of material. *MacRae's Blue Book,* published annually since 1910, consists of several volumes, largely a classified products directory. One volume gives the manufacturers' addresses, while another contains thousands of pages of catalogs from many manufacturers.

Thomas Register of American Manufacturers and Thomas Register Catalog File, published annually since 1905, also has a product arrangement of manufacturers, a list of manufacturers' addresses, plus a list of brand names and trademarks. There are also separate volumes composed of reproductions of company trade catalogs.

VSMF Design Engineering System is an example of one of the compilations of vendors' catalogs and product specification sheets on microfilm cartridges. Arranged by type of product, it covers thousands of products, and it has a monthly updating service.

For most states in the United States there is available a handbook which variously is called a manufacturers' directory, classified business directory, or directory of commerce and industry. Some are available from the State Chambers of Commerce, others from private publishers. Examples are *Directory of Commerce and Industry, State of Delaware,* available from the Delaware State Chamber of Commerce, Wilmington, and the *Indiana Industrial Directory,* published by Manufacturers' News, Inc., Chicago.

There are also directories published on specific types of products and their manufacturers, such as safety equipment, data processing equipment, electronic equipment, and metals. Examples are *Best's Safety Directory: Safety, Industrial Hygiene Security* (biennial), *Chemical Engineering Catalog: The Process Industries' Catalog* (annual), *Computer Directory and Buyers' Guide, Electronic Buyers' Guide* (annual), *Metal Finishing Guidebook Directory* (annual), or *Sweet's Catalog File* (annual). This latter covers machine tools, architectural materials, and plant engineering. Some of the above are published as special issues of journals.

Although the directories must be purchased, the manufacturers' catalogs and specifications often are available free on inquiry to the company by any potential purchasers of the products.

NON-SERIAL DIRECTORIES

An important part of every sci-tech library's collection are directories, which may be easily defined as organized listings of products, firms, people and services. Many directories, particularly those dealing with people, are revised regularly and are routinely acquired as serials on standing order. The *Encyclopedia of Associations, American Men and Women of Science,* and *Ulrich's International Periodical Directory* are three of the most heavily used. Non-serial directories focus on a far more specialized audience and the scope is often on institutions rather than individuals. Two representative non-serial directories are the American Society for Testing and Materials' *Directory of Testing Laboratories* and Richard K. Miller's *Directory of Technical Magazines and Directories.* In each, the body of information is not likely to become significantly outdated over a period of several years and, therefore, does not require frequent revision.

The most important features for any directory to offer are completeness, timeliness, and a functional organization where the information is listed and indexed in a manner that makes it easily accessed. This is best accomplished by an alphabetical listing within subjects.

CONCLUSION

The nature of scientific information plays a distinct role in how it is organized, accessed, and used. Raw data collected in a laboratory notebook, for example, might remain unknown to but a small group in the scientific community if not disseminated through a progress report and recorded in an appropriate handbook. Obviously, the myriad of scientific and technical monographic sources has developed as a way to funnel information into practical, workable categories. With a working knowledge of the types of monographs found in sci-tech libraries, librarians should consult up-to-date guides to the literature for lists of specific titles. Currently, *Science and Engineering Literature: A Guide to Reference Services*, 3rd ed., 1980, by H. Robert Malinowsky and Jeanne M. Richardson is one of the best. Other useful guides to the literature in science fields are: Roger C. Smith, W. Malcolm Reid and Arlene E. Luchsinger's *Smith's Guide to the Literature of the Life Sciences*, 9th ed., 1980; Ellis Mount's *Guide to Basic Information Sources in Engineering*, c. 1976; J. Richard Blanchard and Lois Farrell's *Guide to Sources for Agricultural and Biological Research*, 1981; and G. P. Lilley's *Information Sources in Agriculture and Food Science*, 1981.

REFERENCES

1. Nedwell, D. B.; Brown, C. M., ed. *Sediment microbiology*. London: Academic Press; 1982: p. vii.
2. Henden, Arne A.; Kartchuck, Ronald H. *Astronomical photometry*. New York: Van Nostrand Reinhold Co.; 1982: p. v.
3. Doebler, Paul D. TSM publishers peer into the future–and find it bright. *Publishers Weekly*. 211(18): 26; 1977 May 2.
4. Ingelfinger, Franz J. Shattuck Lecture–The general medical journal: for readers or repositories? *New England Journal of Medicine*. 296 (22); 1260; 1977 June 2.
5. Roland, Charles G.; Kirkpatrick, Richard A. Time lapse between hypothesis publication in the medical sciences. *New England Journal of Medicine*. 292(24): 1276; 1975 June 12.
6. Boyer, Calvin J. *The doctoral disseration as an information source: a study of scientific information flow*. Metuchen, N.J.: Scarecrow Press; 1973. 129 p.

Collection Development in Science and Technology: A Focus on Books

Marianne Cooper

ABSTRACT. This article provides an overview of the evolution and changes that have taken place in collection development in science and technology during the past 25 years. It examines some of the factors that are essential to the understanding of the field. These include the nature of science and technology, the publishing industry, the market place and the role of the librarian. It also takes a long look at the selection process and discusses some of the major selection and evaluation aids available specifically for science and technology. Thoughts on possible future developments are offered in conclusion.

INTRODUCTION

Several changes, both theoretical and practical, have taken place in the field of library management over the past twenty to twenty-five years. They have usually been related to and reflected environmental and societal developments, primarily of an economic, political, and technological nature. Through the prosperous years of the 1960s, for example, aquisition and collection development had been considered interchangeable terms applied to describe the functions of book selection and collection building, as well as the business processes of ordering and purchasing. During these favorable economic conditions expansion and growth were the watchwords in America. Both academic and industrial research were expanding, accompanied by a steady growth in the Gross National Product. Reflecting the general trend, U.S. book production more than doubled during the decade. The availability of funds and the in-

---

Marianne Cooper has a BA degree from Syracuse University and the MLS and DLS degrees from Columbia University School of Library Service. She is Assistant Professor at Queens College, Graduate School of Library and Information Studies, Flushing, NY 11367.

© 1983 by The Haworth Press, Inc. All rights reserved.

creasing publishing output precipitated an unprecedented growth of library collections, necessitating the aquisition of additional space to house the influx of new materials. Librarians were also being forced to devise new methods of weeding and storing the older and "lesser used" segments of their collection to accommodate the new resources.[1]

The decade of the 1970s introduced new economic and political conditions. Recession coupled with inflation and political conservatism needed to be countered with more carefully thought out and business like approaches in library management. Technological advances aided the transformation. Unchecked collection growth had to halt, leading librarians had to critically examine their activities. They began preparing aquisition policy statements and standardizing procedures. Evaluation of collections and services became increasingly significant. The increased application of quantitative measures, systems analysis foremost among them, allowed librarians to break the various functions and processes down into their components while simultaneously pointing out their unity and interdependency.

By the later part of the decade librarians were concentrating on zero base budgeting and no-growth libraries. In this altered atmosphere the realization that collection development is an organized and unified function encompassing planning, policy making, selection, aquisition, evaluation and the maintenance activities of weeding, storage, and preservation as well as resource sharing represented a natural evolution.

A survey of the literature of the field reveals increased general activity from the mid-1970s onward. The annual review article in *Library Resources & Technical Services,* for example, introduced the term "Collection Development" in its title in 1979 for the first time and noted in 1980 that three new textbooks, revisions of two older textbooks, two collections of readings, and a two-volume collection of original papers on various aspects of the subject had been published in 1979, 1980 and early 1981.[2] The literature survey also reveals that there is precious little recent information available on any or all aspects of collection development dealing specifically with problems in science and technology. Cohen published two articles, one in *RQ* in 1973[3] and one in *Library Resources & Technical Services* in 1975,[4] dealing with differing aspects of the topic while Opello and Murdock had a contribution in *College & Research Libraries* in 1976.[5] It should be noted that these authors still spoke of acquisitions as being synonomous with collection development. Additional information related to the topic is scattered through textbooks[6] and monographs.[7] Chen's study,[8] although related to the subject only indirectly, needs to be singled out because it demonstrated the importance of applying quantitative techniques to determining policies in the management of a large academic medical library's collection. Interestingly most of the available resources are devoted to the problems of academic and research libraries; public institutions are second, while special libraries (except for medical and health services) place a distant third.

SCIENCE AND ITS PRODUCERS

Of the many characterizations of science two are pertinent to this discussion. In one respect, science may be viewed as a systematic and methodical search for basic interrelationships between postulated causes and observed events. The focus here is on the process as opposed to the data or facts. Science may also be viewed as a body of knowlege representing the findings of investigations and their many reinterpretations forming the archives of humanity's attempts at quantifying nature. The emphasis here is on the accumulation of data and facts. Either of these approaches accommodates the reality that theories, viewpoints and interpretations have changed in the past, are changing now, and will continue to change in the future. This is, of course, even more true of technology, which Arnold Toynbee, the British historian, called "a bag of tools." In this respect one needs only to consider the evolution of computer technology progressing from mechanical adding machines through vacuum tubes to today's integrated circuit chips.

Scientific research continues to be characterized by two almost contradictory approaches. One trend toward increasing specialization where fewer and fewer researchers are investigating an increasing number of specialities is evident. Conversely, inter- and multidisciplinary research is expanding, relying heavily on international cooperative team problem solving. Researchers, the producers of science, are employed by academic, governmental, and industrial organizations both in research and development. A combination of financial and peer pressures (a major component of the culture of science) makes it imperative for them to be aware of current activities in their fields. At the same time, they also feel obligated, for the same reasons, to disseminate their findings as rapidly and widely as possible, thereby becoming both the producers and the users of information.

A discussion, however brief, of the production and dissemination of science would be incomplete without including an often forgotten intermediary in the science communication/dissemination process. Because of their common interest, background, and language, scholars tend to communicate only with each other. Thus, another professional, the science writer, is often needed to decode and translate the specialists' messages into understandable concepts and relatively jargon-free language for the general public. In this context the science writer becomes the middleman between the producer of science and the consumer of science. His activities encompass both the mass print and broadcast media and frequently expand into the writing of up-to-date lengthier "popularizations" of highly technical subjects.

Because of the emphasis on currency and the need for wide dissemination of scientific research results, scholarly papers published in journals and to some extent technical reports constitute the major components of science's record. The book publishing field, consisting of specialized monographs, treatises, reference sources, textbooks, and works of a general nature, although a sizable industry, plays a secondary role for the practitioner of the field. According to E. J. Crane, however, "books have most important uses. They introduce the novice to the general field of the science or of some part of it, explain new theories in the light of already known facts, and help to coordinate and systematize knowledge . . . Historical works record the development of the science and popular books initiate the public into its mysteries and elicit interest and support"[9]

THE CURRENT PUBLISHING SCENE

The U.S. scholarly publishing arena of the late 1970s and early 1980s differs considerably from earlier but not too distant periods. Changing economic and technological conditions are the prime contributors to the transformation. Mergers and acquisitions in the commercial sector, for example, brought along changes in the size and composition of the industry. Learned and professional societies, the other major book-producing sector in the pure and applied sciences, having concentrated on their journal and serial publications in the past, have begun to branch out into various aspects of book publishing as well. Cooperative efforts between the two sectors are also rather common occurrences. The role of university presses and governmental agencies in the field, although significant, is secondary. There are no exact figures concerning the size of the publishing universe: an estimate of 250-300 organizations seems reasonable.

The steady increase in the volume of publishing is being gradually replaced by a slowdown and an actual decrease in the annual total title output. According to the latest available figures for American books, presented in the October 1, 1982 *Publishers Weekly*,[10] there was a 1.5% decline in the Science category (500-599) from 1979 to 1980 and a 2.3% decline in Technology (600-609, 620-629, 660-699) for the same period. Because of major changes in the counting procedures, however, the final 1981 figures represent an overall increase, instead of the previously projected continued decline for 1981. Thus, in Science the final 1981 figures show an 8.6% increase in the total hardbound and paperbound title output in contrast with the preliminary figures that indicated a sharp 7.9% decline. In Technology, the final computing shows a continued 1% decline as contrasted with the projected 8.6% decrease. The procedural changes, of course, make any meaningful comparisons very difficult.

The average price per hardcover volume in Science, eliminating those priced at $81.00 or more, was $32.67 in 1980. This represents a 17.6% increase over the previous year. Counting all hardcover titles, both domestic and imported, for the same category the average price amounted to $37.45, representing a 22.4% increase over the previous year. In Technology the average price in 1980 came to $33.64, a 20.9% increase over 1979. All the above figures, of course, considerably exceed the annual inflation rates. Although the new average prices in the various subject categories for 1981 have not yet been released because of the previously mentioned procedural changes in Bowker's method of computation, it was reported that escalation of the average per volume price has continued in all subject areas for the year.

Reasons for price increases abound. According to Curtis Benjamin[11] the publishing industry in recent years needed to make up for the unrealistically low book prices of the post World War II period, in addition to being affected by the general inflationary economy of the country. It must also be noted again that science is increasingly characterized by the abundance of small specialized sub and sub-sub disciplines, making the potential market for any new title inherently limited. Thus lack in potential sales volume needs to be compensated for by proportionately higher prices to make the publishing venture economically viable.

THE MARKET PLACE

Publishers of sci/tech books have traditionally considered institutional customers to be their primary targets for major promotional and sales efforts. Academic, research, and special libraries and information centers have formed the core clientele while public and to some extent school libraries followed behind. Although the market for sci/tech publications is small in comparison with the market for publications of general interest, there was a spectacular growth in sci/tech collections in just about all types of libraries during the post World War II period through the early 1970s. Budgets increased to accommodate the demand for information sources in support of a generally expanding research and development effort. The publishing industry (both book, journal and A&I services) expanded to facilitate the dissemination of new findings and research results. For example, new U.S. sci/tech book production grew from 865 titles in 1950 to 3872 titles in 1974.[12] The industrial growth brought along continual price increases, resulting in the steady upward spiral of institutional budgets. The sci/tech portion of most academic library budgets increased both in absolute terms and in relation to other fields.

When the onset of recession halted expansion, retrenchment became the watchword. Library budgets could no longer keep up with cost increases. Since serials and A&I services were the main sources of information for scientists, libraries began shifting funds from monographs to serials to keep services and operations going. The decline in the number of monographs purchased by a medium sized academic library, as shown below, illustrates this.

Year	Number of Titles Purchased
1978/79	604
1979/80	381
1980/81	246
1981/82	227

Individual end users, although obviously the final link in the information transfer chain have been unknown entities, considered by publishers to be hard to reach and difficult to deal with. Major exceptions to the above were publishers of engineering handbooks, since acquiring one's own handbook had been an integral part of an engineer's education. A change in this traditional philosophy, precipitated by the changing economic and technological environment, is however becoming evident.

While institutional customers are still important, the shift in their budget allocations from books to serials and the general decline of their purchasing power is forcing publishers to redirect their efforts to previously disregarded or superficially served segments of the market. These segments include the individual end user, both specialist and layman, and the international arena. In order to gain the attention of individuals many professional and learned societies have, for example, set a two-tier price structure for many of their products: a higher price for institutions and a lower price for individuals. Active and forceful pursuit of international markets, especially in third world countries, is in line with current American business practices in both manufacturing and service industries.

LIBRARY RESOURCES AND THE INTERMEDIARY

In his role as the intermediary between information and its consumers, the librarian has the responsibility of assuring access to and availability of materials for his clients. During the years of growth and expansion of science collections in academic and research libraries this led to an unprecedented degree of accumulation of materials with relatively little regard for budget and space limitations, patterns of use of collections, and the information seeking and use behavior of patrons. Weeding and storage of materials had assumed great importance because of the increased publishing output, the importance of current information, and the relatively high rate of obsolescence of materials in many of the sci/tech fields. During this time many librarians also availed themselves of approval plans and blanket purchase orders in an attempt to maintain economic purchasing and currency of materials. Unlike others, however, industrial special libraries have not generally participated in the great collection expansion phenomenon. Interpretating their institutional goals and objectives more narrowly, they concentrated on the provision of information services thereby following the motto of the Special Libraries Association—"Putting Knowledge to Work."

Conditions have changed and so have professional practices. The 1980s might eventually be referred to as the period of limited or controlled growth. The focus of collection development clearly is planning and policy making in terms of institutional goals and objectives, user needs, fiscal prudence, and cooperative agreements. There is also a renewed interest in weeding.

The importance librarians attach to written collection development statements is demonstrated by their steadily increasing number over the last decade. Magrill[13] notes that libraries of all sizes and types, including school, small academic, academic research, public and special collections, were among those publishing policy statements in 1981. Although the popularity of collection analysis and the search for rationalization of collection building techniques and procedures can clearly be traced to Stanford University's first publication of its statement in 1970, one might be reminded that prior to and since that time science libraries of all types and sizes have been in the forefront of this activity. The author, for example, recalls her involvement in an intensive collection analysis as Columbia University's Chemistry Librarian in the mid-1960s. Industrial special librarians were also engaged in systematizing their approach to acquisition of materials by the late 1960s and early 1970s.[14] Of the various quantitative techniques employed for collection analysis and development, use and user studies have remained popular. There have also been examples of using the computer in the preparation of book selection policies. Columbia University,[15] for example, used the computer to indicate the extent and language of holdings in many different collections. Others have used the computer to establish quantitatively, through analysis of circulation records, which subject fields by class codes are most heavily used. Various statistical methods were then used to assess the collections and note their weaknesses and strengths. The Bell Laboratories Library Network[16] and the National Oceanic and Atmospheric Administration Environmental Research Laboratories Libraries[17] have developed and implemented such techniques.

THE SELECTION PROCESS

"Book selection is an imperfect science at best, if it is a science at all."[18] More importantly, however, it is a serious decision making process whose results have far reaching short and long term consequences. Those charged with the responsibility of selection must be attuned to institutional plans and objectives, user needs and actual patterns of use, the scope, strength, and weaknesses of various subject fields represented in the collection, available human and fiscal resources, and cooperative arrangements, both existing and potential. While book selection may indeed be an imperfect science, when carefully executed it will lead to a collection of high quality instead of merely high quantity.

There are several commonly accepted criteria applicable to the selection of all types of books, including monographs, treatises, and reference works. The order in which they will be discussed is not an indication of priorities since each situation is unique. Consideration of the users, their needs, and the collection as a total picture will assure their most effective use for a particular library.

1. Producers: Authors, Sponsors, and Publishers

The reputation and authority associated with each of these plays an important role in the decision to purchase or eliminate a given title. One learns fairly quickly through experience the identity of respected and well known science authors. Since they do not abound, however, greater attention must sometimes be paid to the reputation of the publisher rather than that of the author. Ascertaining the credentials and background of newcomers or unknowns contributes to the difficulties associated with the decision making process. The decision is easier when professional or learned societies, or governmental agencies sponsor a publication, since its purchase is virtually imperative.

2. Subject

Regardless of the reputation of an author, a sponsor, or a publisher, a work will naturally be excluded if it is totally outside of the scope of a given collection. Assuming, however, that an item is in fact within the scope of the parent organization's interests several factors need to be considered. How extensively, for example, is the organization involved in the field? This might be measured by the number of people working directly in the area or in bordering or related fields. Another measure might be the funds expended for R & D, manufacturing, or other operations. If the subject is not currently "hot," but has been in the past and might be again in the future, one might decide to maintain a limited collection, possibly reference sources only, for continuity. The current strength of the collection in the field, indicated by the number and nature of titles available should be accurately known. Based on a knowledge of institutional goals and objectives one can then assess its adequacy or needs for strengthening.

3. Level of Treatment

Ascertaining the identity of the audience for whom the work is primarily intended is essential. Matching an item with its prospective users is a major factor in the decision making process. Undergraduate level texts and works of a general or "popular" nature would rarely be appropriate for a specialized sci/tech collection, although there frequently is a need for them in public libraries and other collections. Conversely it is occasionally, although not often, the case that a monograph is written for an audience that is more advanced and specialized than the clientele the library serves.

4. Language

English has been the dominant language of science for many years. Recent studies, however, indicate that although it is still the most common language of publication its wide lead, as a percentage of total publications, has been diminishing. It is nevertheless safe to assume that the greatest demand in the U.S. will continue to be for English language materials, allowing the addition of only a few "milestone" foreign language monographs to most collections. Extensive research or storage facilities and/or designated libraries in a network environment will probably serve as resource centers for those with great needs for foreign language material.

5. Age

Since currency of information is essential to most sci/tech fields this criteria is especially significant as the information in most books tends to be outdated by the time they are published. New and revised editions of works already held need special scrutiny to determine the extent and significance of the revisions.

SELECTION AIDS

Keeping abreast of the current sci/tech publishing output and making appropriate choices from this exhaustive universe is no small task. It is this author's contention that collection development and book selection are among the most challenging professional tasks facing librarians today. Monitoring publishers' announcements of forthcoming and/or already published items is usually the first step in the current awareness cycle. These releases, however, cannot be considered as final conclusive statements regarding the titles they are describing. Bibliographic, content, price and time features frequently change. At times, announced books don't even get published. Publishers' annual catalogs, on the other hand, are documents frequently worth saving since they usually present a complete and accurate accounting of material emanating from the various houses.

Library Journal produces a semi-annual classified listing entitled "Scientific, Technical, Medical & Business Books" that combines the expected output of publishers for a limited time period, such as November through February, and groups them according to broad disciplines. There are no annotations or indications of level or intended audience. There is, however, a sufficient amount of descriptive information for ordering purposes.

The annual feature "100 Outstanding Titles for General Collections: Sci-Tech Books of 198.." is a selective classified, annotated compilation prepared by Ellis Mount and Edith Crockett for *Library Journal*. Annotations are evaluative and indicate the level and intended audience. Preceding the listing is a handy assessment of sci/tech publishing events and trends of the year. This compilation, in the March 1 issues, serves as a double feature for some collection developers since it is a selection aid and an evaluative tool. *Library Journal* also publishes occasional special features devoted to information sources in selected sci/tech fields. The January 1, 1981, issue, for example, was devoted to "energy," and there was an "Environment Update" published in the May 1, 1982, issue.

Also keeping the general public in mind, *Science Books and Films* of the American Association for the Advancement of Science provides critical reviews of books, films, video cassettes, and film strips. Being right in step with the times, video cassettes are the latest medium to be added to those reviewed, starting with Volume 18, 1982. This is another selective aid, giving an overall rating, as well as evaluating scope, content, currency, quality, and audience level of all items it includes. It is arranged by DDC classes.

A discussion of book selection aids that concentrate on the needs of the general public would not be complete without mentioning the Carnegie Library of Pittsburgh's annual publication *Science and Technology: A Purchase Guide for Branch and Small Public Libraries.* It is a selective, annotated, classified list (according to LC) from the books received by the library. Interestingly, the number of titles included steadily declined from the high of 1000 in 1978 to 500 in 1981. This source, again, fulfills the dual function of selection and evaluation.

Book reviews appearing in primary journals play an important role in the selection process for specialized collections. They can be found in both discipline oriented and in interdisciplinary publications, including *Physics Today,* the *Journal of the American Chemical Society, Nature, Science,* and the *American Scientist.* Since usually subject specialists prepare them they are evaluative and often critical in nature, thus giving invaluable help to selection officers. Even though *Choice* covers all fields of human endeavor, its short unsigned but comparative assessments in the sci/tech area are valued by many bibliographers of large public and academic libraries. The topical essays, preceding the main section in each issue, are also quite useful as selection and evaluation tools by themselves. The essay entitled "The Ancient and Modern Science: Astronomy" by Margaret Dominy published in September 1981, for example, gave an interesting description of the evolution and development of the field.

Technical Book Review Index provides monthly access to book reviews of new technical, scientific and medical books appearing in 50 trade and technical journals annually. Arranged in broad subject categories about 300 entries are included each month. Besides the bibliographic information each entry contains a usually signed extract from the original review. The ownership of this publication passed from the Special Libraries Association to the JAAD Publishing Company in 1976. Since that time the scope of coverage has noticeably decreased.

The New York Public Library's venerable publication *New Technical Books* is a selective, classified (according to DDC), annotated list describing the Library's new acquisitions in the pure and applied physical sciences. Levels of titles included range from the basic elementary to the complex advanced. English language sources dominate but "important" foreign language items are also reviewed. Annotations usually include indication of content and are signed. Although in some cases this tool can fulfill the dual duty of being a selection and collection evaluation aid, in this author's view, its major strength lies in evaluation because of the frequently lengthy time lag between the date of publication of the book and the date of appearance of the review.

The R. R. Bowker Company's family of trade bibliographies pertaining specifically to science and technology has steadily been increasing over the years. The annual *Scientific & Technical Books and Serials in Print, Scientific, Engineering and Medical Societies Publications in Print* and the latest six volume *Pure & Applied Science Books 1876/1982* are important sources for bibliographic verification, acquisition-ordering and collection development. These are listings on a large scale, aiming for comprehensive coverage, as they define it, without much attempt to guide uninitiated librarians or help them make choices.

FINAL THOUGHTS

Inflation, retrenchment, reevaluation of thinking and procedures, technology, but most importantly change and more change are some of the watchwords that increasingly characterize both the world of publishing and the world of information management and libraries. Librarians faced with escalating prices of resources and with loss of their purchasing power precipitated by an inflationary economy have regularly been shifting their funds from books to serials to keep a semblance of currency in their collections. An additional, but more subtle, change has also been taking place in the management of their collections and their funds. The recency of monographic collections has further been declining because the limited book budgets are frequently spent on the acquisition of reference sources rather than monographs. This, of course, assumes that a combination of an up-to-date reference and serials collection can satisfy immediate, if not long term, user needs in science and technology. The increasing availability of electronic technologies coupled with the funding problems have been creating a more favorable climate for network development. Resource sharing, designated subject collection responsibilities, the availability of local centralized storage facilities have been bringing forth a change in the philosophy of resource management. The primary role of libraries and information centers in the not too distant future will be the provision of availability and accessibility of resources not necessarily their local accumulation.

Shrinking institutional markets and economic realities, including escalating production costs, are forcing the publishing industry also to make changes. There is an increasing tendency to produce shorter press runs in order to avoid accumulating large inventories that tie up their funds. This practice, of course, might create further difficulties for librarians in obtaining desired titles unless orders are placed swiftly. Publishers are also turning increasingly to electronic technologies to help them both with the production and dissemination of their products. Electronic customized data base publishing, especially of reference sources that contain information that is subject to relatively frequent changes, might become a common practice in the not too distant future. It seems obvious then that everybody's work is cut out for them. While in some respects we are retrenching, on the whole our professional horizons are greatly expanding.

REFERENCES

1. Cooper, Marianne. Criteria for weeding of collections. *Library Resources & Technical Services.* 12(3):339-349; 1968 Summer.

2. Magrill, Rose Mary. Collection development and preservation in 1980. *Library Resources & Technical Services.* 25(3):244-266; 1981 July/September.

3. Cohen, Jackson B. Undergraduate science book lists. *RQ* 13: 35-38; 1973 Fall.

4. Cohen, Jackson B. Science acquisitions and book output statistics. *Library Resources & Technical Services.* 19(4): 370-379; 1975 Fall.

5. Opello, Olivia; Murdock, Lindsay. Acquisitions overkill in science collections—and an alternative. *College & Research Libraries.* 37(5): 452-456; 1976 September.

6. Bonk, Wallace J.; Magrill, Rose Mary. *Building library collections.* 5th ed. Metuchen NY: Scarecrow; 1979. Broadus, Robert N. *Selecting materials for libraries.* New York: H. W. Wilson Company; 1981.

7. Osburn, Charles B. *Academic research and library resources.* Westport, CT: Greenwood Press; 1979.

8. Chen, Ching-chih. *Applications of operations research models to libraries.* Cambridge, MA: The M.I.T. Press; 1976.

9. Crane, E. J. et al. *A guide to the literature of chemistry.* New York: Wiley; 1957.

10. Grannis, Chandler B. Statistical report: 1981 domestic. *Publishers Weekly.* 222(14): 40-41; 1982 October 1.

11. Benjamin, Curtis G. The weaving of a tangled economic web. *Publishers Weekly.* 219: 41-45; 1981 April 24.

12. Osburn, op. cit. p. 99.

13. Magrill, Rose Mary. Collection development in 1981, *Library Resources & Technical Services.* 26(3): 240-252; 1982 July/September.

14. Schwartz, James H. Accessibility, browsing and a systematic approach to acquisitions in a chemical research company library. *Special Libraries.* 62: 143-146; 1971 March.

15. Yavarkovsky, J. et al. Computer-based collection development statements for a university library. *ASIS Proceedings.* 10: 240-241; 1973.

16. Spaulding, F. H.; Stanton, R. O. Computer-aided selection in a library network. *Journal of the American Society for Information Science.* 27(5): 269-280; 1976 Sep-Oct.

17. Wenger, C. B. et al. Monograph evaluation for acquisitions in a large research library. *Journal of the American Society for Information Science.* 30(2) 88-92; 1979 March.

18. Lucker, Jay K. Library resources and bibliographic control. *College & Research Libraries.* 40(2): 141-153; 1979 March.

The Acquisition of Monographs in Large Academic Scientific Research Libraries: Current Issues and Problems

Maxine H. Reneker
Suzanne Fedunok

ABSTRACT. This article discusses current issues and problems in the process of acquiring scientific monographs in large academic scientific research libraries. The use and value of monographic material, the broad scope of the collections, the libraries' diverse clientele and the competing demands for resource dollars are described. Approval plans are discussed at length. Cooperative agreements result in faster access to materials at other institutions, cooperative purchase of expensive or little used materials and vendor discounts. Changing technology has implications both for the acquisitions process itself and the formats in which material will be acquired.

A primary issue to be addressed when considering the purchase of monographs for academic scientific research libraries is whether it is necessary and desirable to continue adding material in this format at all. As we contemplate the future of our collections in relation to changes in both the patterns and format of scholarly scientific communication, we must face the possibility that by continuing the purchase of monographs today we may be contributing unwittingly to the obsolescence of our collections. The flow of information may soon pass us by in a torrent of electronic information transfer and

---

Maxine H. Reneker received a BA in Latin, from Carleton College and an MA from the Graduate Library School, University of Chicago. She was a Council on Library Resources Academic Library Management Intern at Columbia in 1980/81. She is currently Chief, Science & Engineering Division, Columbia University Libraries, New York, NY 10027. Suzanne Fedunok is a graduate of Bryn Mawr College and has the MA and AMLS degrees from the University of Michigan. Joining the Columbia University Libraries in 1977, she is Mathematics/Physics Librarian.

© 1983 by The Haworth Press, Inc. All rights reserved.

machine-held data bases, both full text and bibliographic, which can be accessed directly by information brokers, scientific researchers, faculty and students.

Monographs are already widely held to be a secondary source of published scientific information, far surpassed in importance by more rapid means of publication, such as journal literature, preprint collections, and technical reports. In an information age when the growth of knowledge is so great, and the means for widely transmitting and storing it electronically seem to be at hand, why purchase books whose contents are six months to two years old when they reach the shelf and may already be out of date?

In this article we shall build a framework in which answers to this question become clear, for the near term at least. By describing the scope of academic scientific research library collections, the techniques and technologies used to develop and acquire material for them, and the ever-widening context of networks and cooperative arrangements in which they are placed, the need to continue the acquisition of monographic material becomes evident.

NEED TO ACQUIRE MONOGRAPHS

There are many different kinds and uses of monographs in the sciences and the need to acquire these volumes varies from discipline to discipline.

For example, in the earth sciences, which are descriptive in many subdisciplines, stratigraphic and geologic atlases and systematic studies, retrospective as well as current, are necessary to support current research.

The need for monographic materials is paramount in the field of mathematics, where it is not unusual to refer to monographs published in the 1920s and 1930s or earlier.[1] There is great value placed on monographic material in engineering also.[2] Even in physics, which is noted for the importance of current material like preprints, important monographs and treatises such as Landau and Lifshits's *Course on Theoretical Physics* are usually kept in multiple copies. Astronomy places heavy reliance on star atlases. Even in the exploding field of neurosciences, basic texts like Fruton and Simmonds' *General Biochemistry* and Ramón y Cajal's treatise *Manual de histología normal y tecnica micrografica* is still an important reference source.

DEFINITION OF MONOGRAPHS

Denis Grogan devotes several chapters in *Science and Technology: an Introduction to the Literature,* to definitions and examples of specific types of monographs such as directories, yearbooks, treatises, monographs, textbooks, introductions, outlines, and conference proceedings. He characterizes monographs as covering a narrowly-defined single topic, striving however to be comprehensive within its limited subject field. It provides full documentation, emphasizes contemporary knowledge, and "serves in a handy form to draw . . . attention . . . (to) the research results reported, perhaps rather obscurely or inaccessibly, in the primary literature."[3]

In contrast, a textbook aims not to impart information about its subject, but to develop understanding of it. "If the role of the monograph is systematization, the role of the textbook is simplification . . . The success of a textbook depends not on its worth as a source of up-to-the-minute data but on whether its method of presentation enables its users to learn about the subject."[4]

Finally, Grogan quotes E. J. Crane's statement on chemical books which concisely explains the uses of monographs and demonstrates their value.

> They introduce the novice to the general field of the science or of some part of it, explain new theories in the light of already known facts, and help to coordinate and systematize knowledge. They furnish information, exhaustive or not, in a form adapted for quick reference, and guide the searcher back to the original source by means of citations. Historical works record the development of the science, popular books initiate the public into its mysteries and elicit interest and support, and treatises on the various fields . . . give the reader the benefit of the long experience or combined researches of many workers.[5]

In many scientific disciplines, current research work relies more heavily on preprints and journal literature than on monographs and proceedings. However, monographs can present the final form of research announced in preliminary form in abstracts and preprints. They are important to those not in the communication network (the "invisible college") likely to see the data reported in preprints, such as graduate students and faculty switching to new fields or pursuing unfamiliar areas of research. Although researchers come to the library most frequently to read the journals received in the last few days (or hours), they are also found browsing through the monograph collection. The new book display is one of the places researchers always look when they come to the library to find new materials. Conference proceedings especially meet the need for a quick survey of recent results in an unfamiliar field, as does the category of monographs described as review series, or reviews of progress in a subject. These are becoming more and more important as research fronts move ahead at an increasing rate of speed.

SCOPE OF ACADEMIC RESEARCH COLLECTIONS

The mission of an academic library is to identify, acquire, store, and make accessible materials and information needed to support the teaching and research programs of its parent institution. At present a significant portion of this information is published in printed form, in monographs as we have defined them above. While it is true that an increasingly large percentage of expenditures for current materials in large research libraries is channeled to serial budgets, 58% in 1980/81,[6] the remaining 42% still represented over $86,000,000. In the science collections, serials may account for about 70% of the materials budgets. At Columbia University Libraries, approximately 20% of the total expenditures for current materials flow into the sciences (excluding health sciences). The Science and Engineering Division budget for 1982/83 is $675,000, of which $114,000 is budgeted for monographs (not including monographic continuations).

To allocate these monies equitably, the research library must determine what types of management data it will gather and how it will use these data to distribute its resources among the competing needs of the university's programs and clientele.

To understand the extent of this competition, one must comprehend the complexity and diversity of the demand for these resource dollars.[7] Support of research projects totaling tens of millions of dollars, purchase of reserve materials for classes in departments with thousands of undergraduate students, replacement of tens of thousands of volumes of deteriorating materials in those sciences where older material is still heavily used and microforms do not yet provide viable alternatives, and the development of collections of popular treatments of general science on subjects for non-science majors all compete for the monies.

To document their decisions regarding level of support allocated among competing programs and needs, many large research libraries either have formal collection policies or are in the process of formulating them.[8] The need for such documents in building science collections is obvious. With diverse clientele, academic library collections must serve the needs of undergraduates, graduate students, and faculty researchers as well as the public in state supported institutions. Needs are not fixed; new fields are created, departments merge or split, research grants are awarded in new areas and established research projects are completed or terminated by cancellation of the research grant; courses are created or changed, expanded or dropped. The staff responsible for building library collections changes, and the history or rationale behind decisions, as well as the documentation of the decisions themselves, are lost.

The collection development statement must reflect the current needs of users. Discussion is essential with graduate students about their studies and future research interests, with undergraduates about their texts and supplementary readings, with faculty about their research and teaching programs, and with everyone of the above groups about their general or recreational reading in science.

Good selectors will be aware of what grant-funded research is going on in their department, at what dollar figures, how long the grants run, and how much library support is needed both in the short and long term for each project. In this day and age, they must usually represent to the faculty the impossibility of building a permanent comprehensive collection for all research going on at all levels in the department, and they must sell the faculty on the inevitability of sharing resources not only with other departments on campus, but also of relying on interlibrary loans from other library systems.

Selectors must also discover what research is in the proposal stage and begin to assess collection needs at that time, explaining to the faculty that as old research dies and makes way for new projects, the library collection must shift to accommodate it. Research likely to be on a short-term basis, such as that in the hands of graduate students, non-tenured faculty, or short-term project groups, will usually have to get less support than long-term, ongoing projects. Close contact with the faculty about their future plans is essential here. Fortunately, it is the nature of faculties and research programs to build on former strengths, as it is for library collections.

In some departments there is a widening gap developing between the research interests of the senior faculty and the research interests of younger faculty and graduate students. For example, students admitted for an advanced degree in physics may discover that theoretical and high energy particle physics, the well funded and glamorous specialty of many departments in the past, now offers few job openings and therefore little chance to do research, whereas newer areas of applied research such as condensed matter physics seem quite attractive. The challenge of providing library support to the graduate student population can be difficult, especially in those library systems still divided into department libraries, and one must be always on the alert for newly developing areas of research.

It is always important to contact new faculty members about their courses and research interests. New faculty are often hired to broaden the range of courses taught or to bring new knowledge or a new approach to the department. Therefore they may need materials not in the collection plan for the library system. In some cases, they may only be on the faculty for a few years. Nevertheless, it is very important to keep in touch with them: they often have important perceptions about how the present collection differs from others they are familiar with. They can point out gaps in the collection's strong points, as well as signal areas where research is changing and where new subjects are growing. The collection officer must decide in consultation with other members of the departments or faculty library committees whether to develop seriously the collection along these new lines or not.

In the final analysis, however, it is the university administration which determines what academic programs will be supported. Academic officers must communicate these decisions to the library, so that shifts in programs can be met in a timely way by shifts in collection policies. For example, Columbia University recently had to shift resources to support a new computer science department. There was a need to build an instant research-level collection of monographs as well as journal titles in this area. Columbia University Libraries will spend about $20,000 in 1982 for current and retrospective monographs to support its young department. The timely shift of resources is also quite important when programs are to be dropped by the administration. Too often the library is the last to become aware of the demise of a department, so that monies that might have been committed to new and perhaps underfunded programs continue to be spent on moribund ones. On many campuses committees charged with examining university resources and making recommendations for the restructuring of university priorities have produced reports which can serve as bases for changes in the collection development policy. For example, the "Marcus Report" at Columbia makes specific recommendations for additional faculty appointments in various academic departments, endorses interdisciplinary developments in specific fields, and suggests needed changes in the libraries.[9]

TECHNIQUES USED IN ALLOCATION AND EVALUATION

Rational allocation of resource dollars demands information about current rates of publishing; average cost per volume in various disciplines; production of cataloging in major utilities such as CATLINE, OCLC, and RLIN; circulation patterns in the institution's various libraries or by subject discipline; patterns of acquisition by date, country of publication, and discipline; actual expenditures against allocations or projected expenditures; changes in academic programs or in research activity; number of students and the number of courses in various departments; growth rates by discipline or library versus available shelf space; holdings of the collection as measured by the shelflists; acceptability of microforms to clientele; anticipated decrease in collection size due to weeding, deterioration, or theft; and results of user surveys at the institutions.

A great many articles have been published recently concerning techniques of collection evaluation, guidelines for collection size, or projections of acceptable acquisition rates, using most of the various measures outlined above.[10] The Clapp/Jordan formula[11] and the Voigt acquisition rate formula[12] are among the most well-known attempts at rationalization of resource allocations. One of the most elaborate models for "collection control," with applications for the number of titles to be acquired and weeded was described by Sinha and Clelland and applied to the physics book holdings of the Mathematics/Physics Library of the University of Pennsylvania.[13]

However, according to Wilmer Baatz, who conducted a collection development practice survey in 19 ARL libraries in 1977-1978:

> These allocations are, in all cases I believe, based largely on the history of what has gone on before in each library system. The history may be for one year, four or five years, or even up to eight or nine. The experience of the immediate past year is

generally the most significant . . . There have been a few brave efforts to come up with a formula to improve the allocations, but all have discovered that this is indeed a difficult goal to achieve.[14]

It is more likely that the kind of management data described above are used in ad hoc ways by the head science bibliographer or individual selectors. With it, they confirm use, publishing or acquisition patterns observed in day-to-day operations, make informal evaluations of their selection practices, and justify requests for allocations for subsequent years. The use of these kinds of data in individual analyses of collection needs is very important. To the extent that a bibliographer keeps informed of the changes in these variables and ascertains their impact for collection development, he/she will be better able to project and justify budget requests and build collections related to institutional needs and programs.

CURRENT MONOGRAPHS VERSUS OTHER NEEDS

The dollars available for purchase of current research level monographs in the sciences are directly affected by the need to maintain adequate serials collections. With the coming of the new technologies, there will be the further need to transfer some monies away from acquisition and storage of materials and toward the funding of online access to full text journals and bibliographic databases. The storage and archival functions can never totally disappear from the charges of large academic research libraries, howevever, until viable alternate forms of storage to print are created and marketed in a way that makes their distribution to the user more efficient than distribution to, and through, libraries.[15] If that occurs, the functions of an academic librarian will change completely from preserver and accessor, to identifier and retriever.

The need to purchase multiple copies affects the amounts of money available for current research monographs, especially in institutions with many department libraries instead of a combined science library, or with departments which teach large classes requiring access to multiple copies of reserve items.

The need to replace missing and stolen materials cannot be ignored. While the most recent work on a subject is most critical for researchers, they still want to refer constantly, albeit briefly, to a body of older "classics." These titles are often placed in locked or permanent reserve areas. Access is limited unless the titles are kept in multiple copies, some of which are readily accessible.

For much the same reasons, the need to replace deteriorated material by reprints or to fill in retrospective gaps in the collection will also compete with the need to purchase current monographs. In a large academic research library a collection maintained in good condition representing the history of research in scientific subjects is essential, even though current research has moved beyond the results disclosed in these older works. Even the preservation of a fairly complete series of editions of undergraduate textbooks may show the great changes in the field in the past fifty or sixty years. Such a collection may be important to scholars in the history of science. In the field of mathematics the need to preserve and replace monographic materials is even more pressing because the commonly accepted figures for the half-life or currency of materials in science do not apply, and books dating from the turn of the century continue to be of interest to researchers. Finally, because almost all of the materials in what is considered modern science were published on high-acid paper, there is a need to commit funds to convert materials no longer available on paper to microform for storage and preservation. A recent survey of a sample of the Geology collection at Columbia revealed an astounding 56% of the collection in need of rebinding or replacement. Since funds for both rebinding and replacement are budgeted as part of the total Divisional resources allocation, monies to address the need must be diverted from the monograph or the serials budget.

In summary, maintaining an adequate collection of the latest monographs in science may seem like an impossible task, akin to a juggling act. Particularly in larger and older research collections, replacement of deteriorated or stolen titles, purchase of additional copies of texts or classic works for reserve collections, and occasional retrospective buying compete for the same resource dollars as current serials, monographs, abstracts and indexes, and series devoted to current state-of-the-art reviews.

SUPERVISION

Supervision of the collection development function to manage this juggling act is mandatory, particularly in large academic library systems with many branches. A coordinator prepares documents justifying budget requests for the sciences as a whole and insures proper allocation of resources among the departments, keeping institutional priorities in mind.

It is difficult for local department librarians to be objective in the matter of budget allocations and program supports. They are loyal to their local constituents, and often they are regarded more as members of their science departments than as members of the large central library staff. This closeness is desirable in collection development work, but the needs of one department must be balanced with those of other science libraries, not to mention the requirements of the larger library system. There is no pat answer or formula to the problem of the best way to allocate resources. The job of the chief bibliographer is to arrive at a way that seems to work best in his or her situation.

The coordinator also evaluates the selectors on the knowledge and skill they display in building their collections. He or she may initiate user studies throughout the libraries to gather data on the factors described above. The coordinator may become a spokesperson for the sciences on committees developing policy for the entire system or defining it in areas that overlap with the humanities and social sciences. He or she should also be a part of any groups which consider reallocating library resources, either among materials budgets, online tools, or to document delivery services.

NEW TECHNOLOGIES

While the impact of new technologies has been more immediately obvious in its effects on serials, particularly with full text retrieval of journal articles from online data bases already begun on an experimental basis, new technologies have consequences for the development of monograph collections as well.

Online access to the full text of serials and monographs is already at hand. BRS provides full text access to the *Harvard Business Review*.[16] Elsevier plans to provide access to test files of *IRCS Medical Science* and approximately 10-12 biomedical journals such as *Biochimica et Biophysica Acta, Toxicology,* and *Brain Research.* Full text access to certain legal monographs is already available in some libraries, such as Columbia University Law Library.

Even more important in the long run may be the downloading and storage of vast amounts of information on video discs, magnetic tapes, floppy discs and smaller and more capacious chips.

New technologies have potential for addressing the problem of deferred maintenance of large amounts of deteriorating material, and of the replacement of missing material. Libraries are now preparing master negatives when they film material for preservation. Commercial firms such as UMI have for many years produced titles on demand. Under the 1977 RLG Preservation Microfilm Program, 61 titles from Columbia, Yale, NYPL and Harvard were filmed and master negatives prepared from which copies can be produced.

As video disc technology progresses and bibliographic control of master negatives increases, the need to build remote strorage warehouses to accommodate materials weeded out of research science collections may be unnecessary. Libraries can adapt these new advances in information storage and rapid, inexpensive production of on-demand duplicates to supply material as it is requested instead of storing it indefinitely in great quantity.

The purchase of expensive abstracts and indices to the literature must be seriously considered today, knowing they are or will soon be in machine readable form and directly accessible online. In some cases, it may no longer be necessary to buy printed indices and abstracts and their various cumulations when large files of online data bases are directly searchable using Boolean logic operators. Publishers, experiencing decreasing revenues from the sale of printed indices, have now begun to increase the cost of access to the online form of the indices when the subscriber does not also purchase the printed ones. However, studies have shown that librarians and users prefer printed indices to online ones for certain types of searches.[17] The form in which selectors purchase or refrain from purchasing materials now, and the shift of resources from printed to online text, must be considered as part of the entire resource allocation process.

SPEED IS OF THE ESSENCE

Were any science collector financially able to purchase all the new materials he or she wanted to add to the collection, there is the question in many of the largest library systems of whether the material could be acquired, processed, and made available on the shelf to science researchers in a short enough time to justify its purchase in the first place. This problem is severe in the sciences where material goes rapidly out of date. Some libraries are exploring the establishment of quotas or priorities; brief, or minimal level, cataloging; and the setting of new collection policies to limit the number and kind of materials acquired. In 1978, Magrill and East commented on this trend toward greater selectivity in new acquisitions and greater efficiency in procedures.[18] Although these trends were perhaps stimulated initially by budgetary considerations, increasing emphasis on evaluating the quality of library collections in terms of availability rather than total holdings, combined with increasing backlogs in technical processing, have forced libraries to be more selective and efficient, even after budgetary pressures have relaxed.

Book selectors in the sciences must be aware of the pressure of time in doing their work and place orders in the most efficient manner. In library systems where there are levels of priority in processing and cataloging, science materials can be given high priority.

Another way to speed delivery of science materials is to use the services of an approval plan, in effect delegating the initial selection of materials to a vendor and circumventing the first stage of the delay, the order process. Approval plans will be discussed at some length in the following section because they are effective in solving the important problem of timely delivery of materials.

APPROVAL PLANS

There are several major approval plan dealers used by academic science libraries, e.g., Ballen Booksellers International, Coutts Library Services, Baker and Taylor Co., and Blackwell-North America Inc., and a growing number of publishers, e.g., Springer-Verlag, Birkhauser, Van Nostrand-Reinhold, now offer approval plans to customers. All of the companies offer slightly different programs, which should be compared and evaluated thoroughly before beginning an approval program or selecting among the vendors. Discounts, availability of reports, invoicing and profiling routines, forms used, service, reliablility, accuracy of bibliographic citation, speed in delivering materials, and problem solving ability should be taken into account.[19]

Apart from the time and labor saved at the technical processing end, there are numerous collection development advantages to approval plans. Jennifer S. Cargill and Brian Alley point out the advantages in *Practical approval plan management.*[20] These are summarized and expanded, both positively and negatively, as follows:

1. The library may obtain current titles while they are readily available. Rapid acquisition is an important consideration in the sciences, where print runs are usually very short.

2. Books are provided quickly, often before the reviews appear and before they are listed in bibliographies. This may be a disadvantage for selectors not well versed in highly technical subjects if they do not have the advice of faculty and researchers to assist in the selection process. One study has shown that under an approval plan only 14% of titles identified from reviews had to be firm ordered, because over half were already in the collection and another 20%

eventually arrived on approval.[21] While many vendors claim to supply books within a month or two of publication, titles often have not been received in the library by the time they are received and cataloged in the RLIN database.[22]

3. The collection profile can range from comprehensive to specific and be tailored to suit the buyer's needs. Most vendors will advise new customers to think of the profile in terms of excluding certain types and levels and subjects of material, rather than attempting to describe everything that must be included. The distinction between a blanket order plan which is inclusive and material nonreturnable, and an approval plan, must be clear to both the vendor and customer. Most vendors will advise that it is not worthwhile to attempt an approval plan unless one is collecting at close to comprehensive levels in at least one or two broad subjects. The profiles must be reviewed regularly with the vendor and brought up to date with changes in the research and instructional program.

4. Firm orders and standing orders may be "interfaced" with the plan, or even handled by the same vendor, to avoid unnecessary duplicates. Duplicates will still come, must be accepted or returned, and procedures developed to attempt to minimize them.

5. Books may be returned without advance authorization, provided they are returned within a specified time. If the profile is good, theoretically there will be few rejects. When the number of rejects exceeds a critical percentage, e.g., 10-20%, it is time to reevaluate the dealer's selection processes and to change the library's profile.

6. Time savings can be realized by reducing the number of catalogs and reviews read, preorder searches and verifications done, vendor selections made, orders prepared and filed. These functions will not be eliminated entirely, and in fact most libraries end up with a duplicate set of files for approval plan materials. They may find it necessary to scan catalogs and reviews to monitor the approval plan's effectiveness and to do preorder searching of firm orders to avoid duplication.

Those libraries with access to RLIN or OCLC have a tool for double checking on the delivery of materials on the approval plan; another way is to monitor *New Technical Books,* or *Technical Book Review Index,* publishers' catalogs, or the acquisitions list of a library of similar size and collection policy. Most vendors will accept "claims" on their approval plans; however, some of them regard such claims as firm orders, and will not allow credit on returns.

7. The preparation of a profile may result in a more organized

approach to the collection, especially where there is not yet a formal collection development policy or where there is no unified science library.

8. Selection is done with the book in hand. Faculty members as well as librarians may scan the complete work. This close inspection of titles, especially when done by faculty members, can result in what vendors may view as an overly high refusal rate. However, it certainly can make the selection process more efficient by reducing the number of books acquired which will be of little value to the collection.

9. The vendor can supply useful statistical reports based on approval plan records for the individual library as well as data broken down by subject area for all materials supplied under the plan.[23]

10. The vendor can supply form slips for the books not sent, annotated to show the reason they were out of the profile. In this way, selectors gather some idea of the larger universe of current science monographs. The slips may be used later to respond to faculty requests for these titles or checked against book reviews or accession lists from other libraries with similar collections.

A good science bibliographer will want to monitor the effectiveness of the plan and be prepared to make changes and head off problems at an early date. If a high enough percentage of desired titles is not coming through fast enough under the plan, he or she may decide to drop the plan altogether.

In the sciences, new books within the accepted profile must be received within a few months of publication; there must be agreement about what is inside and what is outside the profile; and there must be a willingness to accept occasional deviations from it. The virtue of an approval plan is that one gets to see the books before purchasing them. One sign that an approval plan is slipping is the reception of increasing numbers of ''form selections'' when the librarian believes the books should have been sent.

In the large and complex university, with its hundreds of scientists and scores of research projects, it is essential that the science selectors know or be able to find out quickly what monographs are needed and be able to communicate this information to the approval plan vendor. Vendors tend to have a broader view of the kind and number of books that must be bought by any respectable science collection than the selectors and faculty themselves often do. This makes for a sometimes uneasy partnership, especially in times of shrinking budgets.

As more and more individual science publishers develop their own approval plans, and if publishers and the central processing units of large library systems improve their capacity to deliver materials quickly and invoice them accurately, approval plans with publishers may become more attractive than they are at present. Now the costs of invoicing and problem solving for a variety of acquisition sources often create headaches and force librarians in large systems to look more favorably toward a single approval plan dealer.

FIRM ORDERS

An approval plan cannot be expected to bring in everything that is needed in a large academic science research collection. Even in library systems using approval plans very successfully, the placing of firm orders still accounts for a large percentage of orders. Some libraries allocate fifty percent of the monograph budget to the approval plan and reserve the rest for other purchases.[24] In other libraries this percentage may be considerably less. Firm orders are necessary for books not supplied by the plan: publications of learned and professional societies; publications of those U.S. publishers not handled by the approval plan vendor; foreign titles; reprints and replacements; retrospective buying to fill gaps in the collection; orders for microforms; and reserve materials.

GIFTS

Libraries can usually rely on gifts to fill some of the gaps made by thefts and loss of out-of-print materials, to add to a collection of undergraduate textbooks, to obtain multiple copies of popular books, or to replace deteriorating materials. However, since they cannot predict what will be offered or when it might arrive, there is no way to rely in any consistent way on gifts as a regular source of current monographs. One may canvass the faculty regularly for desk copies and save money for other kinds of purchases. The library may make it known in the departments that gifts of any kind are welcome, with the understanding that not all donated material will go into the collection. Finally, the selector should be aware of any large privately owned faculty libraries in the department. He or she should be prepared to request as a gift the odd replacement volume, and prepare the ground for the donation of the entire collection upon the retirement of the faculty member or the dissolution of the research laboratory.

Gifts from faculty are also important if not critical in those literatures like physics which value proceedings of meetings. These are often impossible to get after a few months, particularly the foreign ones. To obtain a volume later, the library must solicit it from the faculty in the interests of making the information accessible and the library's collection complete.

In the future, online lists of gift books available within a library consortium will improve the chances of finding needed out-of-print material.

SCIENCE FOR THE NON-SCIENTIST

More and more, universities have come to realize their commitment to interest students in science and to educate non-scientists in the nature of science and scientific research. Young students must be found to become the scientists and researchers of the future. Recent studies have shown an alarming drop in the number of mathematics and science teachers being trained in universities and colleges,[25] as well as a low level of "scientific literacy" in the college-educated population.

To meet the need for general science material addressed to the non-specialist in the field, book selectors must be able to make good choices among the growing number of popular books on science. They must select monographs based on accurate reporting of valid scientific method. A collection of monographs dealing with questions of current scientific interest and controversy can enable members of the university community to understand the rapid changes brought about by new scientific and technological developments and to evaluate the issues of public policy raised by them.

COOPERATIVE AGREEMENTS

Shared access to bibliographic data bases enables libraries to quickly identify and request titles held at other institutions and to benefit from their acquisition and cataloging records. Cooperative agreements linked to fast and dependable document delivery services enable the cooperating libraries to reduce duplication yet continue to meet the needs of scientists for that kind of material that is only occasionally requested, is peripheral to research at that institution, or is too expensive. More than one recent study has pointed out the high degree of duplication of titles among branch library collections and of duplication among members of consortia.[26]

Under a cooperative agreement the responsibility for building comprehensive collections in given subjects might be assigned to certain libraries, e.g., for certain continents in geology collections, or certain classes in botany. In the New York area, cooperative agreements among Columbia, the New York Botanical Garden and the American Museum of Natural History divide responsibilities for such areas as general geology and micropaleontology to Columbia, botany to the Botanical Garden and vertebrate and invertebrate paleontology to the Museum, with shared access agreements and delivery service to make the agreements viable.

To coordinate collection development among its members, the Research Libraries Group has recently completed work on a collection conspectus based on the LC classification scheme in the physical sciences (QA-QD) giving for each section the current and retrospective collection level at each reporting institution. This information is available online and will be updated at regular intervals. RLG may make assignments for prime collecting responsibility to those libraries which report strong holdings in a particular area. The libraries accepting this responsibility agree to maintain their collection at a research level.

Other shared resource programs pool money for the purchase of expensive items, or coordinate purchases to avoid costly duplications. In the New York area the Metropolitan Reference and Research Library Agency (METRO) initiated a cooperative acquisitions program in 1972. The METRO libraries, who voluntarily participate, share the cost of expensive infrequently used reference and research material. Unfortunately, science materials represent a very small percentage of the titles purchased as part of the program.[27] In Colorado cooperative agreement among the members of the Colorado Alliance of Research Libraries led several years ago to the cancellation of some of their subscriptions to Gmelin. A CARL committee, the Colorado Organization for Library Acquisitions, simultaneously spent $11,000 to complete holdings at one library. Use patterns throughout the state did not support multiple subscriptions to this expensive tool.

A third type of cooperative agreement was described by Lindsey. He reported that a consortium of college libraries in North Carolina receive across-the-board discounts from book jobbers on firm orders by negotiating as a unit with jobbers, who are attracted by the combined potential purchasing power of the member libraries.[28]

As consortia and networks develop online acquisition systems and agreements for collecting responsiblity in certain areas, selectors at an individual academic library can make decisions to purchase titles and record them in the central database of the consortium or network. As jobbers offer online ordering and fund accounting[29] libraries can transmit the order electronically to the vendor's order files. Such innovations speed the receipt of orders and facilitate selection decisions at other libraries in the network on a broad scale.

Library funding agencies are looking most favorably at proposals for projects inputting records into the bibliographic utilities or showing evidence of cooperation among libraries to preserve, identify, catalog and describe collections of similar materials. They are thereby more accessible to other institutions, who no longer have to include them in the scope of their collection policies.

CONCLUSION

The middle of the last decade was a difficult time for building library collections. Serials budgets were severly cut in many large systems, and monograph budgets similarly curtailed. The effects of these unhappy cutbacks on monograph collections in the sciences are still being felt, despite the conventional wisdom about the short half life of materials in science collections. Whereas journals not purchased at that time are generally still available in microform or photocopies of articles in them can be readily borrowed on interlibrary loan, many important monographs of that period are now out of print and are expensive and difficult to purchase. Some are hard to get on interlibrary loan because of their scarcity. Before making decisions to support serials at the expense of monograph buying, libraries must consider that, at the present level of technology, there is no guarantee a specific monograph not bought today will be available on-demand in the future.

In discussing current issues and problems in buying monographs for large academic scientific research libraries, we have reviewed the scope of academic science library collections, methods of acquiring monographs for them, the cooperative settings in which development of the collections occurs, and the importance of monographs to these collections. The theme of the impact of new technologies runs through the discussion. How long the print format will dominate our collections and the process of information transfer is unknown. Rapid increase in efficiencies of storage technology, with related cost decreases, may quickly bring about full text storage of information in machine-held data bases. As a precursor of future trends, the Elsevier Medical Information Retrieval System contains the full text of some of Sanders medical textbooks.

For the near future however, Stuart Forth's prediction will hold: "the book and the journal will not go away. On the contrary, both are proliferating as never before, and access to computerized data bases, combined with new fields of research results in requests for more new books and journals, not less."[30]

As the information demands of our users accelerate and available dollars decline or remain stable, we will need to face hard decisions. Recent figures on U.S. book production indicate that although the number of books in the sciences is going down, prices continue to rise.[31] How shall we allocate resource dollars for monographs among competing research and institution programs, and among alternative means of access to them? The purchase and storage of printed monographs on-site in our libraries will no longer remain the only option. Fast access to borrowed print or microfilm copies via cooperative agreements to fill a specific request, purchase of on-demand copies from master negatives or electronically stored data, or access online to the full text of a monograph may soon limit systematic purchase of print copies to subjects and titles for which there is high and immediate projected use.

NOTES

1. Garfield, Eugene. The 200 "pure" mathematicians most cited in 1978 and 1979, including a list of most-cited publications for the top 100. *Current Contents*. (36):5-14; 1982 September 6.

2. Kriz, Harry M. Subscriptions vs. books in a constant dollar budget. *College & Research Libraries*. 39(2): 105-109; 1978 March.

3. Grogan, Denis. *Science and technology: an introduction to the literature.* 4th ed. London: Linnet Books & Clive Bingley; 1982: Chapter 7, esp. p. 101-103.

4. Ibid. pp. 105-106.

5. Crane, E. J. (and others). *A guide to the literature of chemistry.* 2d ed. New York: Wiley; 1957: p. 11.

6. Figure based on 42% of the total monies for current acquisitions less binding reported in Mandell, Carol A. and Johnson, Mary P. comps. *ARL Statistics 1980-81: A compilation of statistics from one hundred and thirteen members of the Association of Research Libraries.* Washington, D.C.; 1982. p. 6, 19.

7. For an excellent treatment of collection development in large academic libraries, see Magrill, Rose Mary and East, Mona. Collection development in large university libraries in:

Harris, Michael H. *Advances in Librarianship, Vol. 8.* New York: Academic Press, 1978. p. 2-54. and Baatz, William H. Collection development in 19 libraries of the Association of Research Libraries. *Library Acquisitions: Practice & Theory.* 2(2): 85-131; 1978. For a general treatment of collection development in Science, see Mount, Ellis. *University science and engineering libraries, their operation, collections and facilities.* Westport, CT: Greenwood Press; 1975: Chapter 5: Library Collections, p. 50-71

8. Baatz, *op.cit.* p. 96. There is an indication that about half the 19 university libraries he studied had developed policies which were generally being followed.

9. Report of the Presidential Commission on Academic Priorities in the Humanities and Sciences. Columbia University, 1979 December.

10. See for example Bonn, G. S. Evaluation of collection. *Library Trends.* 22(3):265-304; 1974 January, and: Wenger, Charles B., et al. Monograph evaluation for acquisition in a large research library. *Journal of the American Society for Information Science.* 30(3): 88-92; March 1979, and Knightly, John J. Library collection and academic curricula: quantitative relationships. *College & Research Libraries.* 36(4): 295-301; 1975 July. For an excellent bibliography on collection evaluation see: Nisonger, Thomas E. An annotated bibliography of items relating to collection evaluation in academic libraries, 1969-1981. *College & Research Libraries.* 43(4): 300-311; 1982 July.

11. Clapp, Verner W.; Jordan, Robert T., Quantitative criteria for adequacy of academic library collections. *College & Research Libraries.* 26(5): 371-380; 1965 September.

12. Voight, Melvin John. Acquisition rates in university libraries. *College & Research Libraries.* 36(4): 263-271; 1975 July. See also: Hodowanec, George V. An acquisition rate model for academic libraries. *College & Research Libraries.* 39(6): 439-447; 1978 November for predictive values of books to be added based on multiple regression analysis.

13. Sinha, Bani K.; Clelland, R. C. Application of a collection-control model for scientific libraries. *Journal of the American Society for Information Science.* 27(5-6): 370-327; 1976 September-October.

14. Baatz, *op. cit.,* p. 87.

15. See the paper: Di Gennaro, Richard. Libraries, technology and the information marketplace. *Library Journal.* 107(11): 1045-1054; 1982 June 1 for his perspective on the library as the principal market for certain new technological developments.

16. See *BRS Bulletin.* 6(8): 1; 1982 August.

17. See, for example: Childs, Susan; Carmels, Michael. Effect of online services on purchase of a printed index. *ASLIB Proceedings.* 33(9): 351-356; 1981 September.

18. Magrill and East, *op. cit.*

19. See: Grant, Joan; Perelmuter, Susan. Vendor performance evaluation. *Journal of American Librarianship.* 4(5): 366-367; 1978 November for a comparison of three dealers on three of these factors.

20. Cargill, Jennifer S.; Alley, Brian. *Practical approval plan management.* Phoenix, AZ: Oryx Press; 1979.

21. Hulbert, Linda Ann and Curry, David Steward. Evaluation of an approval plan. *College & Research Libraries.* 39(6): 485-491; 1978 November.

22. Informal studies at Columbia University show that virtually all books received from its approval plan dealer already have records in the RLIN database at the time of their receipt at Columbia.

23. See, for example: Blackwell North America, Inc. *Approval program coverage and cost study 1981/82,* various paging, for a detailed subject breakdown of the number of titles supplied, and their related costs, in 1980/81 and 1981/82.

24. Posey, Edwin D. The approval plan experience of an Engineering Library in *Shaping Library Collections for the 80's.* Fourth International Conference on Approval Plans and Collection Development. Milwaukee, 1979. Edited by Peter Speyers-Duran and Thomas Mann, Jr. Phoenix, AZ: Oryx Press; 1980.

25. Worthy, Ward. Classroom users in science and math. *Chemical & Engineering News.* 60(29): 9-16; 1982 July 19.

26. Knightly, *op. cit.*
27. New York Metropolitan Reference and Research Library Agency. Cooperative Acquisitions Program. *A dictionary catalog of materials purchased through the cooperative acquisitions program 1972-79.* p. iii.
28. Lindsey, Jonathan A. Vendor discounts to libraries in a consortium. *Library Acquisitions: Practice and Theory.* 5(3-4): 147-152; 1981.
29. Alessi, Dana L. Book jobbers, here today, gone tomorrow? *Library Acquisitions: Practice and Theory.* 5(1): 21-25; 1981.
30. Forth, Stuart. Myths and realities: the politics of library administration. *University of Michigan School of Library Science Alumni in Residence Program.* Ann Arbor, MI: University of Michigan, School of Library Science; 1981: p. 16.
31. *Bowker Annual of Library and Book Trade Information.* 27th ed. New York: Bowker; 1982: p. 385, 388, 400.

Sources of Information Used by Selectors in Four Medical School Libraries for Collection Development

Beatrice Kovacs

ABSTRACT. The collection development practices in four medical school libraries are analyzed in terms of sources of information used by selectors for identification of materials to be purchased for the collections. Materials to be purchased include monographs, serials, periodicals, and audiovisuals. Data and conclusions are based on interviews with selectors in the four medical school libraries studied.

INTRODUCTION

The development of collections, and the proper and efficient use of budgetary funds for such collections, has been a concern for medical or health science librarians for many years. In 1937, for example, Hunt[1] expressed concern about the selection of periodical titles when funds are limited, and in 1976, Truelson[2] discussed the problem of faltering budgets and the proliferation in publishing, with some suggestions for selection criteria to help in the selection process. As technology improved and new methods of information dissemination were developed, such as the computerized bibliographic and knowledge base systems currently available, the health science library began to move toward a goal identified by Darling[3] in 1974—the goal of conversion to a communications center working with all kinds of informational materials for all types of health profession users. The informational materials needed in the modern health science library include the traditional forms (books and

---

Beatrice Kovacs received an AB from Syracuse University, an MLS from Rutgers University and is pursuing a DLS at Columbia University. She is currently Consultant for Program Development at Read-More Publications, Inc., New York, NY, and Visiting Instructor at Pratt Institute Graduate School of Library Science, Brooklyn, NY.

© 1983 by The Haworth Press, Inc. All rights reserved.

periodicals), and non-traditional forms, examples of which are online databases containing bibliographic information or factual material (the Hepatitis Database developed by the Lister Hill National Center for Biomedical Communications offers factual data online), and audiovisual learning materials, such as those available from The National Medical Audiovisual Center (currently developing the Human Genetics Knowledge Base videodisc project).

The problem then arises for the health science library to obtain and disseminate the information contained in the variety of formats available in the marketplace, and additionally to remain within the confines of the budget. How do the selectors choose those materials which will provide relevant information to meet the needs of their users? What sources of information are relied upon by selectors to identify materials for purchase for the library collections?

ACCESS TO THE SCIENTIFIC LITERATURE

With the increase in publishing of scientific research, particularly the abundance of scientific proceedings and conference reports, technical papers, and new serials which have been created in recent years, there has been increased concern among librarians regarding access to information about these materials. Over the years, health science librarians have had several sources which analyzed the periodical literature and arranged the citations by subject headings; notable examples are *Index Medicus, Excerpta Medica, Biological Abstracts,* and *Chemical Abstracts.* The indexing and abstracting services were often slow and very expensive, but necessary to have. With the improvements in technology which allowed computer technology to become a major information source in libraries, there came the opportunity to have not only online access to the periodical literature in the sciences, but also to enable commercial firms to create and produce new indexing and abstracting sources for use in libraries. These sources are presenting more current information than had been possible in the past. New kinds of indices were developed, such as the Institute of Scientific Information's citation indices, and new services such as their tearsheet service by which librarians could receive computer printouts of citations according to profiles and order reprints of articles. As access to the periodical literature improved, demand for enlarged periodical collections increased and libraries were unable to meet these demands within their budgets. Medical and health science libraries began to develop strong interlibrary cooperation in order to meet the needs of their users, and the National Library of Medicine created the Regional Medical Library Program, a national network for resource-sharing and interlibrary loans.

Although some of the online bibliographic databases include a limited number of monographs, there is still difficulty in identifying new imprints as soon as they are published. Many librarians feel that they cannot wait until the reviewing services analyze recently published monographs, and they use sources such as *Weekly Record, Library Journal,* Library of Congress proofslips, or other similar sources for current information. In the medical sciences, there are sources such as *Current Contents* and the National Library of Medicine proofsheets which have been found useful. Some medical librarians have felt that a well-developed profile makes an approval plan the most timely and effective way to identify and buy the latest in monographic materials for the library. Unfortunately, many medical and health sciences libraries have budgets which are too small to support a cost-effective approval plan.

Sources of information on audiovisuals are limited. There is the *Health Sciences Videolog,* and there are catalogs produced by the National Medical Audiovisual Center, as well as several general audiovisual catalogs and indexing services, but some librarians do not have these sources available to them. In some cases, locally-produced software constitute the major components of the audiovisual collection. Local audiovisual consortia seem to be good sources for information on software and hardware for collections.

MEDICAL SCHOOL LIBRARIES

There are a variety of health sciences libraries in the United States. Health sciences libraries can be located in private or public hospitals, or they can be created to serve the informational need of members of a society for one of the health professions. There are governmental health sciences libraries, such as those serving the Veteran's Administration, or the library which has the greatest influence on health science library services, the National Library of Medicine. There are also commercial health sciences libraries, such as those located in pharmaceutical companies and other commercial establishments which deal in products or services for health sciences practitioners or the public. Additionally, there are the libraries which serve the educational, research and, often, patient care needs of institutions of higher education called medical school or health sciences universities. Although the information disseminated by these types of libraries is the same, the needs of each individual library differ because of the concerns of its parent institution or the needs of its users.

For the purposes of this paper, medical school and health sciences university libraries were chosen for study. The purpose of the study was to identify the sources used by the selectors in medical school libraries to determine what materials would be purchased for the collections in the library. Four medical school or health sciences university libraries indicated willingness to participate in the study. Anonymity was guaranteed, so the libraries will be designated as Library A through Library D. All four libraries are located in the same geographical area, with the same resources available to each, including resource collections, networks, consortia, and commercial firms such as vendors, serials jobbers, etc. All four libraries have access to the OCLC database and its services, and all provide bibliographic online search services for their users through the MEDLARS system, BRS, SDC, and other databases.

Library A

Library A is located on the campus of a medical school which is part of a private university system. This university has many campuses in other locations in the state, and serves undergraduate and graduate students in the humanities, arts, social and physical sciences, and other areas of endeavor. The medical school library has a collection of over 100,000 volumes and more than 1,500 periodical subscriptions. Until recently, Library A was a member of an audiovisual consortium which purchased medical audiovisual materials, but due to financial reasons, the consortium membership had to be dropped. Therefore, the library is beginning to develop an audiovisual collection of its own. The current acquisitions budget is over $250,000 for monographs, periodicals, serials, and audiovisuals which are needed to serve the needs of the School of Medicine, programs in nursing and the allied health sciences, and the teaching hospital, located on the medical campus.

In the 1970s, a collection development policy was created that defined the areas of development for the collection and the areas of exclusion, and included a list of approved aids to selection. This written policy continues to be the basis for selection decisions in the library.

Selection decisions are made by designated members of the Technical Services Department of the library. The person with primary responsibility for collection development is the Head of Cataloging, who is aided in these duties by the Acquisitions Assistant. The Head of Cataloging receives all requests for purchase of materials from the faculty, staff, and students of the institution, and passes on those to be purchased to the Acquisitions Assistant for ordering. Aside from the order duties, the Acquisitions Assistant is responsible for the Approval Plan shipments, involving the checking of the shipments, analysis of the monographs and serials received, and the return of unwanted materials. Over the years, Library A has developed a referral system within the institution, which involves a panel of subject experts on the faculty of the medical school who are regularly asked to evaluate any materials received that cover their areas of expertise. The recommendations of these experts are followed, and rejected materials are returned to the vendor. When items of great expense are requested or received on approval, the Director of the Library is consulted.

In addition to evaluation of the Approval Plan shipments, the Head of Cataloging, the Acquisitions Assistant, and other library faculty regularly scan a variety of sources for information on materials which should be purchased for the library's collections. These sources of information include bibliographies, course reading lists, publishers' ads, library acquisitions lists, reviews, and some abstracting and indexing services, as can be seen in the Tables 1 and 2.

Library B

Library B is a medical center library which is part of a state university system. The medical center houses schools of medicine, nursing allied health sciences, and graduate studies; other campuses throughout the state offer a variety of programs for students. Library B has a collection of almost 250,000 volumes, and nearly 1,500 current periodical subscriptions. A few years ago, the state university system gave Library B $30,000 seed money to begin an audiovisual collection, and the Audiovisual Department of the library has been expanding rapidly. The current acquisitions budget for monographs, periodicals, serials, and audiovisuals is over $250,000.

There is no written collection development policy for the library. The selection of printed materials for the collection is done by the

TABLE I.-- Sources of Information Used in Four Medical School Libraries for Collection Development.

Source of Information	Library A Yes	Library A No	Library B Yes	Library B No	Library C Yes	Library C No	Library D Yes	Library D No
Abstracting and Indexing Services:								
Biological Abstracts		N		N		N		N
Chemical Abstracts		N		N		N		N
Current Contents								
Clinical Practice	Y			N		N		N
Life Sciences	Y		Y			N	Y	
Excerpta Medica		N		N		N		N
Index Medicus		N		N		N		N
Science Citation Index		N		N		N		N
Commercial sources:								
Approval books	Y			N		N		N
Approval lists	Y			N		N		N
Publishers' ads	Y		Y		Y		Y	
Publishers' catalogs	Y		Y		Y		Y	
Publishers' newsletters	Y		Y		Y		Y	
Series lists	Y		Y		Y		Y	
Vendor catalogs	Y			N	Y		Y	
Vendor newsletters	Y		Y		Y		Y	
***On-line services:**								
AVLINE		N		N		N		N
CATLINE		N		N		N		N
BRS	Y			N		N		N
Lockheed	Y			N		N		N
MEDLINE	Y			N		N		N
OCLC	Y			N		N		N
PHILSOM	Y			N		N		N
RLIN		N		N		N		N
SDC	Y			N		N		N

*Library A reported that its Reference Department regularly scanned these sources and forwarded purchase recommendations.

TABLE 1.-- Continued.

Source of Information	Library A		Library B		Library C		Library D	
	Yes	No	Yes	No	Yes	No	Yes	No
Scientific journals:								
British Medical Journal		N		N	Y			N
Journal of the American Medical Association	Y			N	Y		Y	
Lancet		N		N	Y			
Nature	Y			N		N	Y	
New England Journal of Medicine	Y			N	Y			N
Quarterly Review of Biology and Medicine	Y			N		N		
Science	Y			N	Y		Y	
Scientific American	Y			N		N	Y	N
Sources by or for librarians:								
Acquisitions lists	Y		Y		Y		Y	
Bibliographies	Y		Y		Y		Y	
Books in Print	Y			N		N		
"Brandon" list **	Y		Y			N		N
Bulletin of the Medical Library Association	Y			N		N	Y	
Cumulative Book Index		N		N		N		
Library Journal	Y			N	Y		Y	
National Library of Medicine Catalog		N		N		N		N
National Library of Medicine Proofsheets	Y			N		N		N
Publisher's Weekly	Y			N	Y		Y	
Special Libraries	Y			N	Y		Y	

**Brandon, Alfred N. and Hill, Dorothy R., "Selected List of Books and Journals for the Small Medical Library." This list is published annually in the Bulletin of the Medical Library Association.

59

TABLE 2.—Other Sources of Information Used.

Source of Information	Library A	Library B	Library C	Library D
Other sources:	Course reading lists Interlibrary loans *American Journal of Nursing* *Choice* *College and Research Libraries* *Information Hotline* *New Titles in Bioethics*	Interlibrary loans Local audio-visual libraries Local nursing audiovisual consortium *AAAS Science Books and Films* *Health Science Videolog* *Video Source Book*	Interlibrary loans Library of Congress proofslips Medical center bookstore	Interlibrary loans *American Libraries* *College and Research Libraries* *Information Retrieval and Library Automation* *Library of Congress Information Bulletin* *Library Resources and Technical Services* *Library Trends* *MEDOC* *Monthly Catalog* *National Library of Medicine News*

Head of Public Services, who has complete control of the monographic materials ordered, with the Technical Services staff handling the orders. Periodicals selection is done by a small committee comprised of the Head of Public Services, the Head of Technical Services, and the Director. This committee meets irregularly to discuss titles to be added, and titles to be dropped from the collection. Serials and periodical check-in and processing are handled by the Technical Services department. The members of the Reference Department often recommend materials which are needed for the Reference collection, and the Audiovisual Librarian selects for the Audiovisual collection.

The sources for information used by the selectors at Library B may also be seen in Tables 1 and 2. The main sources of information are publishers' ads, newsletters, and catalogs, vendor newsletters, bibliographies, library acquisitions lists, and a variety of audiovisual sources.

Library C

The medical center campus in which Library C is located is part of a private university system that has a number of campuses in a small geographical area of the state. Other campuses offer programs in the humanities, arts, social and physical sciences, and other subjects, and all are within easy commuting distance from the others. Library C has a collection of over 100,000 volumes and more than 1,500 current periodical subscriptions, with an acquisitions budget of over $200,000 for monographs, periodicals, and serials. There is no audiovisual collection in Library C.

There is no written collection development policy for the library. The selection of materials for the library is done by the Director of the library, with recommendations from members of the Reference Department. The Director has full authority over what is ordered, and sees every request. Those approved for purchase are then sent to the Order Clerk in the Technical Services Department.

A number of sources are scanned by the members of the Reference Department, who then mark those items which they think would be useful for the collections. The Director examines those items brought to his attention by the other librarians, and makes the final selection decisions. The major sources of information for selection are *Weekly Record,* Library of Congress proofslips, publishers' ads, newsletters, and catalogs, vendor newsletters, and library acquisitions lists. (See Tables 1 and 2.)

Library D

Library D is the library for a small school which is not part of a university system. The medical school had some financial difficulties until recently, and the budget for the library has started to increase in the last few years. There are degree programs in medicine and graduate studies, but none in other areas of the health professions. The medical school does not have its own hospital, but there are over 30 local hospitals which are affiliated with the school and provide clinical experience for the students. The library's collection is over 100,000 volumes, and there are over 1,000 current periodical subscriptions. The library also has a very small audiovisual collection. The total acquisitions budget for the library is over $150,000 for monographs, periodicals, serials, and audiovisuals.

There is no written collection development policy for the library, although there are plans to create one in the near future. Selection decisions for the collections are made by the Director of the library, and the Assistant Director, with recommendations from the Reference Department and from the Serials Librarian. Once the selections are approved for purchase, the Assistant Director types and sends the orders; there is a lack of personnel to handle the order procedures. The library has been unable to fill positions due to a lack of funds.

There is a wide variety of sources used by the selectors in Library D to identify materials for purchase for their collections. *Weekly Record, Library Journal,* and many other periodicals are scanned, as well as publishers' ads, newsletters, and catalogs, vendor newsletters, and library acquisitions lists. These and other sources are listed in the Tables.

FINDINGS AND CONCLUSION

The four medical school libraries studied presented a variety of organizational structures within differing institutional frameworks. The library collections vary in size and emphasis, some with audiovisual collections, some without. All selectors within these libraries have the same sources for information available, as well as the same resource collections nearby. It is interesting to note the similarities, as well as the differences, in the preferred sources of information used by the selectors to identify materials for purchase for the collections.

All selectors scanned and selected materials from publishers' ads, publishers' newsletters, publishers' catalogs, and vendor newsletters, as well as lists of series volumes. Three of the four libraries' selectors regularly scanned vendor catalogs, also. Only one library participated in an approval plan, with which the selectors were satisfied, but they continued to scan other sources to insure that no necessary materials were overlooked.

Of sources of information for collection development which were created by or for librarians, library acquisitions lists and bibliographies were examined by selectors in all four libraries. Selectors in three of the four libraries read the reviews in *Library Journal* and *Special Libraries,* as well as the listings of currently published books in *Weekly Record.* The "Brandon" list was checked by selectors in three of the four libraries to assure that the collections had the materials listed. None of the selectors found *Cumulative Book Index* or the *National Library of Medicine Catalog* helpful for the selection process, although were used in the verification process.

Reviews of new materials which appeared in the *Journal of the American Medical Association* and *Science* were checked by selectors in three of the four libraries, and selectors in two libraries regularly scanned the reviews in *Nature, New England Journal of Medicine,* and *Scientific American.* A variety of other scientific journals were chosen by individual selectors as sources of information, as can be seen in the Tables.

The only abstracting or indexing service found useful by selectors was *Current Contents,* the Life Sciences issues being examined by selectors in three of the four libraries.

None of the selectors searched the online data bases for information on newly published materials for purchase, although the Reference Department of one library did analyze searches done for patrons and forwarded recommendations for purchase to the selectors. The selectors in all four libraries did, however, search the OCLC data base for holdings statements on materials which were considered either expensive or peripheral to their collections. If the item was held in an area library, the selectors would reconsider their decision for purchase. This, the selectors felt, enabled them to more effectively disburse their budgetary funds while avoiding unnecessary duplication of some types of materials within the area.

In conclusion, it appears that selectors prefer to make selection decisions from information created by the commercial firms, such as publishers and vendors, and from library acquisitions lists and bibliographies, rather than from any online data bases or most of the abstracting and indexing services. Also prevalent was the use of *Weekly Record* in three of the four libraries, although it is not geared primarily to the physical or health sciences. Many selectors felt that there is no one source for information, since the field of health information is so broad and complex. Therefore, in order to canvas as many titles as possible, it is necessary to use general sources, as well as select scientific publications, to identify materials for the medical school library's collections. Since health science collections must be as up-to-date as possible, selectors tended to ignore those publications which contained information about titles which were more than a few months old, including the sources produced by the National Library of Medicine.

REFERENCES

1. Hunt, Judith Wallen. Periodicals for the small bio-medical and clinical library. *Library Quarterly* 7:121-140; 1937 January.

2. Truelson, Stanley D., Jr. Selecting for health sciences library collections when budgets falter. *Bulletin of the Medical Library Association* 64(2):187-195; 1976 April.

3. Darling, Louise. Changes in information delivery since 1960 in health science libraries. *Library Trends* 23(1):31-62; 1974 July.

A Brief Study of Unaffiliated Research Level Monograph Authors

Robert G. Krupp

ABSTRACT. Presents results of a survey of more than 600 sci-tech research monographs, published late in 1981 and early in 1982, to determine those in which the affiliation of the author was given somewhere within the publications. Possible reasons for the lack of identification are offered.

The lack of author affiliation in connection with publications, especially monographs, can precipitate a rather puzzling experience. To then determine such affiliation can be frustrating, irritating, and time consuming. There are two immediately obvious reasons for needing an author's affiliation: (1) to be able to contact that individual if there are questions or comments about the work; and (2) to establish immediate, if not preliminary, credibility of the author. Reviewers, for example, have a great interest in this as do faculty selecting works for their courses and, of course, librarians with selection responsibilities.

As to why an author's affiliation would not be noted may not be an easy question to answer. For those pondering this matter a variety of answers are possible: (1) not discussed between author and publisher; (2) not thought important by either party; (3) not wanted by the author; (4) forbidden by the author's employers for a number of hidden reasons; and (5) possibly (but hopefully not) an author being ashamed of his affiliation. No doubt there are others, but regardless, the lack of affiliation identification will usually cause readers to cast a jaundiced eye in the direction of such a work.

It should be noted, however, that in many instances, though affiliation is not given with the author's name on the title page, affilia-

---

Mr. Krupp was, until his recent retirement, Chief of the Science and Technology Research Center of the New York Public Library. His current address is 7 Maple Terrace, Maplewood, NJ 07040.

© 1983 by The Haworth Press, Inc. All rights reserved.

tion may be provided on the verso of the title page camouflaged in fine print, or noted at the conclusion of the preface or introductory comments, or even buried in the text itself. Actually these kinds of cases cannot be counted as a lack of affiliation identification, but they certainly can escalate frustration on the reader's part.

The use of abbreviations such as a string of initials representing affiliation may be a set so unique so as to be immediately unidentifiable (e.g., government units, industrial organizations) and thus be only slightly removed from being no affiliation at all.

In order to examine this phenomenon (if only superficially) six sets of randomly chosen works were reviewed with this problem in mind. However, the titles were of those only in the English language (but not limited to United States imprints and including translations) on the physical sciences and related technologies, and published during late 1981 and early 1982. (See Table I.)

Of the 630 titles selected, 72% were strict monographs and after screening out those works which were deemed not to be at a research level (choices which were admittedly somewhat subjective but probably adequate for this short study) it was determined that for 20.4% of monographs at the research level no author affiliation was found. It was interesting to note too that of the monographs identified as texts, a startling 46.4% (See Table II) were without author affiliation, although the number of texts within the whole sample amounted to only 4.4% (or 6.2% of only the monographs).

To those not particularly concerned with this problem, 20 monographs out of 100 may not seem too great for author affiliation lacks, and indeed the percentage is less than was originally imagined (25%) to be the case. Nevertheless when one is faced with the need-to-know affiliation, even the somewhat lower percentage can cause the problem to truly balloon and indeed supports the rationale for this survey.

Though the sample used was relatively small, it was interesting to note that of authors who had their works published in the United States and who had affiliations cited, 80% of these affiliations were from outside the United States. (Distributors were not called publishers.) Why this is so is indeed another matter (beyond the scope of this survey) but could well involve situations where renumeration plays a role, or the speed of publication, the quality of the published product, supposed prestige enhancement, or refusal of publication in homelands. The 20% residue, that is, authors published in the United States and with United States affiliations, seems a rather scant one.

TABLE I
MONOGRAPHS

Random Groups of Titles	Monographs No.	%	Research Level No.	%	No Affiliation No.	%
132	106	80.3	99	93.4	19	19.2
112	90	80.4	84	93.3	20	23.8
119	89	74.8	85	95.5	14	16.5
99	73	73.7	72	98.6	4	5.6
122	70	57.4	62	88.6	19	30.6
46	26	56.5	24	92.3	11	45.8
630	454	72.1	426	93.8	87	20.4

TABLE II
TEXTS

Texts	No Affiliation No.	%
7	2	28.6
6	4	66.7
4	3	75.0
1	0	0
8	3	37.5
2	1	50.0
28	13	46.4

But returning to the affiliation lack problem, the solution is childishly obvious: authors and publishers should use affiliations even if authors are retired or unemployed (then use at least a home city). Accomplishment though is another matter and to reach that end development may travel the broad road of good intentions but, unfortunately studded with the potholes of resistance, ignorance, legal entanglements, and an outright flaunting of the needs of faculties, librarians, and readers in general by such authors and/or publishers.

The Monograph is Not Endangered —But Its Package is Changing

Gary Craig

ABSTRACT. The question "what is the future of the monograph in libraries?" is critically important to scientific and technical publishers such as Wiley, because libraries historically have provided a stable base of sales which made it possible to publish a professional title at a price within the reach of the individual reader. Factors such as shrinking acquisitions budgets, increasing numbers of new book titles, and competition from alternate forms of information delivery are forcing publishers to apply increasingly conservative standards to selecting new manuscripts and to consider whether the "monographic package" is the optimal choice for the title's true audience.

Publishing—whether commercial or "not-for-profit"—is a *business*. As in any business, a product is created, an audience is identified, an approach is designed to make the audience aware of the product, and members of the audience make individual decisions to part with something of value in order to obtain the product. All these things must happen, whether the "product" is a book, a candy bar or an airplane.

But there are differences which make published "products" unique. Though our product is packaged, by tradition, in an object called a *book,* the product is not the book itself. The product is the body of ideas or information expressed in the graphic symbols we use to share the ideas among each other, and the book evolved as an inexpensive, portable, and effective instrument for storing and transmitting these small "databases."

Gary Craig is Manager of Library Sales and Services at John Wiley & Sons, Inc., 605 Third Avenue, New York, NY 10158. He is also the Marketing Manager for Wiley's electronic publishing program. Mr. Craig received his degree from the University of Missouri.

© 1983 by The Haworth Press, Inc. All rights reserved.

ESSENTIAL PRODUCT CHARACTERISTICS

Audience

Commonly an author's purpose in creating a manuscript is to disseminate a body of ideas or information to a large number of people in a comparatively short span of time. The publisher supplies the delivery system, through a combination of editorial participation (to make the ideas understandable to the audience being addressed) and marketing expertise (which brings the existence of the book to the attention of its audience and informs the members of that audience how they may obtain it). Obviously the packaging of a product can make a sizeable impact upon the audience being addressed, but the audience's chief interest, in the final analysis, is in the package's contents.

Durability

Publishers and their customers are, of course, concerned with the durability of their product. The physical package has a finite life which depends in part on the publisher's manufacturing specifications and quality control procedures and in part on the physical laws of the universe, especially "entropy," which dictates that all things proceed towards coming apart rather than remaining intact. Often the life span of the package has a direct effect on the life of the ideas, because a durable package ensures that the ideas will be available for transmittal during a long period of time. In most cases, an author is very concerned that the ideas in his/her book remain available for a long time.

Portability

The monograph is a classic example of a design which addresses both the nature and function of the product in terms of the product's users, and does so in a compact form which is easily carried, shipped, stored, and even augmented by the user through personal notes in the margins (of his/her *own* copy, we hope!). This package has remained the optimum choice for the product in terms of the existing market environment.

EVOLUTION OF THE ORGANISM

For many decades, the monographic book has been accepted as the standard means to house and transmit the idea product to its audience, and this central fact has grown into a complex administrative organism of publishing, marketing, distribution, acquisition, storage, cataloging, indexing, and numerous other activities directly related to the physical package of the product. Clearly, libraries and publishers are a primary component of this organism, and our separate actions in pursuing our interests have institutionalized our systems and procedures into very stable patterns having an air of "permanence."

But the information organism has been growing and changing. Some of its less essential characteristics have begun to fade, and others are taking on new prominence. As with any evolving being, these changes do not originate in the organism, but are brought about by changes in the organism's environment.

Wiley started publishing 175 years ago, and published only a handful of new titles that first year. Last year, we published 764 new titles. We have published new titles on this scale for many years, and expect to continue doing so, in order to maintain freshness and diversity in our product mix. However, libraries' resources, taken as a whole, have not grown as quickly as publishers' new title output. Simple arithmetic tells us, therefore, that we publishers can sell fewer and fewer copies of each new title in our "library market" each year.

Seeing the growing disparity between new title output and library budgets, the wise publisher begins looking outside the traditional library community to discover additional audiences. For some of these newly discovered audiences, a bound printed monograph is not the "best" package, and here begins the process of balancing the interests of the old and new audiences to achieve the combination which will meet the author's and publisher's needs. For some of these needs, the monograph remains the package of choice; for others, the monograph will be the base, and alternative formats will be created for the additional audiences; for still others, the monograph will be supplanted by a format which is more effective in delivering the information to its audience.

A CASE STUDY IN EVOLUTION

Here is a specific example of the way a specific Wiley product evolved to serve the needs of its audience.

In 1969 Wiley published a book called *Atlas of Mass Spectral Data*. This book is a collection of mass spectral values against which the readings from a mass spectrometer are matched in order to identify unknown compounds. At the time of its publication, the book was unique in its ability to meet the need for this kind of information, and we sold 561 copies that first year.

However, the scientists who use this kind of information do not content themselves with a simple lookup. The match is seldom exact, and additional analysis involving statistical techniques is necessary in order to determine a level of confidence in the identification of the compound. With increasing access to the power of computers, the scientists using this information created programs to perform the elaborate calculations. The problem, of course, is that the values needed for the calculation were resident in a printed book, and laborous effort was needed to transform them to a form usable to the machine. A still further complication was that the existing body of mass spectral values was constantly growing, making manual analysis increasingly cumbersome.

To bridge this gap, we also offered the product on magnetic computer tape. Now the information could be read directly into a computer, and the product could be constantly up-to-date. Judging by the sales patterns of the book product and the tape versions, we made a valid decision in terms of the authors' needs and the needs of the customers who were using the information; the tape product rapidly surpassed the book in sales, and today we sell the tape product (which has grown from 6000 spectra to approximately 70,000 spectra) almost exclusively, though the 1974 edition of the book remains in print and sells in nominal quantities each year.

It is not difficult to project the example to cover other configurations of product and audience better served by a format other than a printed monograph.

By fulfilling our obligations to authors and product audiences, we inevitably find ourselves in situations where the change of format affects the library community directly. The effect may be the removal of the librarian, an intermediary, and the substitution of a direct relationship between the information producer and the customer, the substitution of intermediaries in an entirely different industry (in this case, the venders of mass spectrometry equipment), or evolution on the part of the library towards the role of an electronic information provider.

COSTS VS. REVENUES

We cannot express surprise at this direction of development, since we have witnessed a parallel phenomenon, the sale of books and journals in microform formats. As costs of warehousing rise beyond a level which an individual title can support through sales, a publisher moves toward a decision to reduce the inventory level or relinquish the title as an active product.

One means to do so, of course, is to simply declare the book out-of-print and devote the company's resources to other products. Appealing as this course of action is from a business management standpoint, some vital interests are compromised by such a move.

By removing the title from the marketplace, we foreclose its availability to certain readers who may not yet have had a chance to purchase it, and thereby thwart a portion of the author's purpose in writing the book. We also work against the needs of our library customers, who may not yet have had an opportunity to buy the book because of budget timing, delayed reviews, or a host of other reasons. A publisher cannot survive by creating ill will among authors and customers, and must exercise great restraint in taking an action as final as declaring a title out-of-print.

There are numerous avenues open to the publisher who wants to keep a book alive, and these options have evolved naturally because all publishers have similar needs and problems. As each set of problems was addressed, a specific change occurred in the way publishers and libraries had been accustomed to transacting business with each other. Some of these options are described briefly below.

Reprint Houses

There are many functions which a small company can perform more effieciently than a large publishing house, and this fact is the basis for the existence of the many fine reprint publishers which comprise an important component of our marketplace. A small company does not have to cover the overhead costs of a large plant and staff. Further, since a major part of a book's expense is the cost of bringing it through the stages of manuscript, editorial, production and manufacturing, and finally producing the first printed copy, a reprint house spared these costs can afford to inventory and market a title in much smaller quantities than would be profitable for a larger house. A reprint house typically has lower fulfillment costs, since smaller quantities require a less elaborate system of inventory management. The difference is important particularly to the library marketplace, where much of the business consists of orders for single copies; this type of order is notoriously expensive for a large operation to handle at a profit.

The reprint publishers identified an important need: the desire by authors, publishers and book buyers that a book be available for purchase until a substantial part of its potential audience has been reached. Extending the book's time of exposure to potential buyers is one way of achieving this objective.

Non-Book Formats

What happens when a book's turnover is insufficient to support a level of sales which would be profitable even for a reprint house? We know from experience that a certain number of copies remain to be sold after the initial selling effort. We also know that a technological or philosophical shift can create a brand new market for a title years after its prime market has been saturated. Besides, most publishers will go to considerable lengths to prevent the expiration of a product whose existence is the result of the creative energies of so many individuals.

Yet—as states initially—publishing is a business, and inflation, Thor decisions, and other business conditions attach very high costs to keeping books in our warehouses in anticipation of renewed sales life.

One answer is microform publishing, which can store a book product and recreate it in an exact ratio to demand. Even though the original "packaging" has been sacrificed, the original idea product remains. To a customer who purchases a microform or photocopied edition, the content rather than the book package has determined the product's value to that customer. New technologies of machine-readable storage and laser printing promise increasing levels of quality for this kind of edition.

And the microform offers an additional advantage to the library customer, an advantage which parallels the cost savings which accrue to the publisher. Because the microform occupies very little physical space, the librarian who must budget a finite amount of shelf space is spared the painful decision to eliminate an important work from a collection because the number of clients using it is small. This benefit has expanded to an unanticipated degree with the advent of books on videodisc and computer tape, which can store and deliver even larger amounts of information in even smaller spaces.

THE INFORMATION IMPLOSION

The seemingly uncontrolled proliferation of data and information has introduced mass storage techniques into the publishing process.

However, this same information volume continually turns in upon itself as well, an implosion process whose result is the creation of finer and finer subdivisions and subspecialities, areas in which bodies of information can find audiences. Sometimes these audiences are smaller than those we would expect for traditional print products.

While past publishing methods limited the degree to which these information needs could be met, the techniques developed for the "information explosion" now offer the means to produce and disseminate book products in small quantities. We may expect to see more and more primary publishing taking on an "on demand" character, and our increasing willingness to forego certain traditional physical characteristics of our monograph products will actually expand the potential number of such products.

With the start-up investment reduced, more and more authors can expect to find publishers willing to provide an outlet for their works. And while the publishers are modifying their marketing and distribution methods to handle this changed mixture of products, libraries must face the related challenge of modifying traditional acquisition and circulation methods to accommodate the changing mix of formats in their collections and to make this variety of information products accessible to their clients.

These changes are not trivial; they constitute an upheaval of an environment in which most of us have grown up. As the process of change continues, we will surely see some publishers vanish and some libraries disappear or become other kinds of information entities. But through all of this, we should see monographs continue to flourish and find their audiences, and the publishing and library institutions which survive and which come into existence in response to this changed environment will be working in an atmosphere of discovery and change, evolving the new shape of the way ideas take on life through being disseminated and preserving those ideas beyond the limits allowed them by our traditional "book package."

The extended example used throughout this paper has been evolution, but perhaps "maturation" more accurately describes what has been happening. We—publishers, libraries, and individual information users—are simply learning to see beyond the physical limitations of the information products we produce, circulate, and use. By broadening our view of the options available for meeting our information distribution responsibilities, we are led with increasing frequency to the technologies used as a matter of course by other industries as tools to increase their effectiveness. Neither our existence nor the existence of our information product has been called into question by these developments; we are, however, being asked to apply some important professional judgements to the ways we meet our goals, and to modify our methodologies to meet the needs of our marketplace.

NEW REFERENCE WORKS IN SCIENCE AND TECHNOLOGY

Janice W. Bain, Editor

Reviewers for this column are: Carmela Carbone, (CC), Engineering Societies Library, New York, NY; David Smith, (DS), Technical Library, Bell Laboratories, Naperville, IL; David A. Tykoson, (DT), Science Library, Miami University, Oxford, OH; and, Barbara Walcott, (BW), Health Sciences Library, Columbia University, New York, NY.

ENGINEERING

Balachandran, Sarojini. *Directory of publishing sources: the researcher's guide to jounals in engineering and technology.* New York: Wiley; 1982. 343 p. $27.50. ISBN 0-471-09200-2.

This directory is intended to help identify the most appropriate vehicle for the publication of research results emanating from engineering or related technologies research. The compiler has identified nearly 300 of the most widely used scholarly journals in engineering, published mostly in English. The compilation includes not only journals published by well-known commercial publishers but also those of professional associations. The directory is arranged alphabetically by the title of the journal, and, in some instances, by the institutional publisher. For each journal the following information is provided: publisher; scope and content; type of acceptable contribution; manuscript submission procedure; style guide; and, the compiler's survey results. The survey information includes number of referees used; time taken for the refereeing process; availability of referees' comments; acceptance rate for manuscripts; turnover time; and, percentage of invited manuscripts. Omitted from the information provided are the usual data such as frequency, price, editor's name, etc., which can be obtained from conventional periodical directories. The last section contains a detailed subject index providing key words used either in the title of the journal or in its scope and contents section. (CC)

GERIATRICS

Robbins, Alan S. (and others), eds. *Geriatric medicine: an education resource guide.* Cambridge, MA: Ballinger; 1981. 446p. $32.50. ISBN 0-88410-728-0.

As interest in geriatrics increases, so does the demand for information on educational programs and materials in the field. This compendium, produced by a team of medical educators at UCLA under contract to the Veterans Administration, is designed to fill that need. It is divided into six main sections. The first consists of detailed descriptions of existing and planned training programs offered by medical schools and other institutions. Continuing medical education programs are included, as well as some programs and courses in related areas, such as dentistry. Books, journal articles, and audiovisual materials in geriatrics and medical gerontology are reviewed in the next three sections. The bibliography of journal articles recommended by educators in the field is arranged by broad subject. Since both the books and audiovisuals are critically reviewed in some depth, this section would be valuable in developing a collection in geriatrics. The fifth part of the book is a compendium of behavioral objectives for levels of medical education as rated by 72 experts in the U.S., Canada, and the U.K. Three of the appendixes are actually indexes to the programs and materials listings. In the other appendixes the methodology is described and samples of the data collection instruments used in compiling this work are provided. (BW)

INFORMATION SCIENCES

Henderson, Fay; Rosenau, Fred., eds. *Information sources 1982-83: the annual directory of the Information Industry Association.* Washington, D.C.: The Information Industry Association; 1982. 319 p. $37.50 ISBN 0-942744-00-0.

This is the seventh edition of the IIA's annual membership directory. It is fairly well designed and includes four sections. The first section is an alphabetical listing of member firms and basically consists of one and two page advertisements which describe the services they offer. The members vary in size from AT&T and IBM to various publishing houses, such as John Wiley and Frost & Sullivan, to numerous small consulting firms. Each listing contains phone numbers and addresses. The second section is a membership roster that is brief and primarily useful for identifying the various operating units within a corporate entity which are not listed separately in the previous section. The third section identifies international offices and trading partners of member firms on a country-by-country basis. This section could be particularly valuable for those seeking information from within a remote nation. The last section is an extensive index which includes a "names and numbers" section. The next edition will be published in the Spring of 1983. (DS)

LIFE SCIENCES

Uleck, Ronald B., ed. *Life sciences jobs handbook.* Gaithersburg, MD: R. B. Uleck Associates; 1979, supplement 1981. ISBN 0-937562-01-7.

In these career-minded times, a great deal of pressure is put on students to go into fields in which it is easy to find a job. This handbook helps deal with this pressure for students of the life sciences, providing a wealth of information on how and where to find jobs in this field. Included are a variety of sources such as a list of life science periodicals with job advertisements in various fields, a list of newspapers from major cities which include job ads, a description of professional organizations with placement services, government and state agencies employing life scientists and consulting and industrial firms. Each section also contains job search strategy hints to help make the most of the information given. The 1981 supplement keeps the handbook current by updating each section. This source will be helpful for job-seekers and for career development collections. (DT)

MEDICINE

Zeitak, G.; Berman, F., eds. *Directory of international and national medical and related societies.* Elmsford Park, NY: Pergamon Press; 1982. 389 p. $70.00. ISBN 0-82-027991-0.

The editors of this directory believe that it is the first listing of both national and international societies in medicine, veterinary medicine, psychiatry, and allied fields. It includes over 4000 professional and voluntary societies. The information provided was gathered by questionnaire, and entries vary in length according to the amount of information available. The shortest consist only of the name, address, and subject area of the organization. The most complete entries also provide telephone number, cable and telex addresses, number of members, future meetings, and titles of society publications. International societies are grouped together; other organizations are listed by country. The whole directory is accessible through country, subject, and society name indexes, the last including former names and native language names (when not in English). (BW)

METALS AND MATERIALS

Walton, Charles F., ed. *Iron castings handbook.* 3d ed. Des Plaines, IL.; Iron Castings Society, Inc.; 1981. 831 p. $27.50.

The third edition of the *Iron castings handbook,* written primarily for castings users, presents useful and authoritative information for those involved in component design, materials specification, casting processing, and purchasing. It can also serve as a reference book for engineering schools and foundries even though the details of production technology are not covered. This edition presents new information and data on properties, metallurgy, heat treatment, welding, and machining procedures. Complete information on all cast irons is given, covering the range of gray, malleable, ductile, alloy, white, and compacted graphite irons. Values are presented in both conventional and international metric (SI) units of measure. A glossary of terms is included. (CC)

MICROCOMPUTERS

Chandor, Anthony. *Facts on file dictionary of microcomputers.* New York, N.Y.: Facts on File; 1981. 184p. $14.95. ISBN 0-87196-597-6.

This dictionary is relatively inexpensive and easy to use. Several definitions are often provided for the same entry which facilitates understanding of its usage. However, the failure to indicate a preferred definition limits the dictionary's function as an authority. Although completed in 1980 the information will probably remain fairly timely since the vocabulary of the microcomputer world is rather well established. (DS)

Graham, John; Wyland, Roy, eds. *International microcomputer software directory.* Los Angeles: Imprint Software; 1981. $29.95. ISBN 0-907352-03-0.

This comprehensive directory—which defines a microcomputer as using 8-16 bit words and having 128K or less memory—is a rather ambitious attempt to provide a guide to this fast growing industry. The authors even suggest that their coding system might turn into an industry standard. There are three main sections which allow the user to access the directory information by machine, subject, or software house. Several useful appendixes such as a glossary and especially a table of machines and operating systems by microprocessors. Look for improvements in future editions which will quite possibly make this an invaluable addition to any reference collection. (DS)

PETROLEUM

Langenkamp, Robert D., ed. *The illustrated petroleum reference dictionary.* 2d ed. Tulsa: PennWell Publishing Co.; 1982. 583 p. $37.50. ISBN 0-87814-160-X.

The second edition of this dictionary has been considerably enlarged. It contains more than 3000 entries and a great number of additional illustrations to aid in understanding the often colorful expressions used in the increasingly multinational petroleum industry. In addition to the dictionary section, the book includes *Universal conversion factors,* compiled and edited by Steven Gerolde, and the Desk & Derrick Club's *Standard oil abbreviator.* These sections are both very useful. The abbreviations probably could not be found in the standard dictionaries of abbreviations. The conversion factors are those pertinent to the petroleum industry and are extensive and detailed. (CC)

STATISTICS

Encyclopedia of statistical sciences. New York: Wiley; 1982- ISBN 0-471-05546-8 (v.1).

This is the first of an eight volume reference work in statistics which has as its stated purpose the provision of "information about an extensive selection of topics concerned with statistical methods in various more or less statistical fields of activity." The editors concentrate on topics of importance during the last quarter century along with those of historical importance. Entries are arranged alphabetically and vary in length from a few sentences to many pages. Most have bibliographies and all have cross references to related articles. The intellectual level ranges from highly technical for the most specific topics to very technical for the most specific topics to very general for the broader ones. An unusual feature is separate entries for the major journals in statistics, with the history and contents of the journals explained. The serial publication of the remaining seven volumes may cause some frustration as there are cross references to articles that do not yet exist and the material in the later volumes will undoubtedly be more current than that in the earlier volumes. Despite these minor inconveniences, this encyclopedia will become the standard reference in statistics in the years to come. (DT)

U.S. GOVERNMENT—INFORMATION SOURCES

Newman, Michelle M., ed. *Washington information handbook.* Washington, DC: Washington Researchers; 1982. 347p. $65.00. ISBN 0-934940-12-6.

It goes without saying that the federal government is one of the world's largest sources of information, most of which is free or costs very little. This reference work is the key to that storehouse and provides a lucid outline of just what is available relevant to science and technology and exactly how to get it. Certainly the information available relevant to science and technology is staggering, but the scope of this treasure extends to virtually every field of endeavor. This volume is intended as a companion to the *Researchers' guide to Washington experts,* which attempts to keep tabs on 10,000 government experts. People often prove to be the most useful resources, but lists of individual authorities simply change too quickly, thus it is easier to approach the federal government through structured, agency listings. This workbook covers every branch of government and will save its buyer more than the purchase price in phone calls alone. (DS)

SCI-TECH ONLINE

Ellen Nagle, Editor

DATABASE NEWS

Computer Information Online

Several databases covering different aspects of the computer industry have been added recently.

Microcomputer Index contains citations to the literature on the use of microcomputers in business, education and the home. Magazine articles, as well as software and hardware reviews, new product announcements, and book reviews are included. The file is produced by Microcomputer Information Services and covers 1981 to the present. *Microcomputer Index* contains approximately 10,000 records and is updated monthly with about 700 records. Available as File 233 from DIALOG, the cost of searching is $45 per connect hour and $.15 for each full record printed offline.

Another new DIALOG file, *International Software Database (ISD)*, is offered as File 232. *ISD* contains information about computer software available from software vendors throughout the world. Each program listing in *ISD* includes a full description, date of release, compatible systems, minimum memory required, update and source code availability, distribution medium and price. Vendor information includes address, phone number, payment terms, and distributors. The *ISD* contains approximately 10,000 records and is reloaded monthly. The cost of searching *ISD* is $60 per connect hour and $.15 per full record printed offline.

BRS has added *RICE (Resources in Computer Education)*, a new source of information about computer education and resources. Produced by the Northwest Regional Educational Laboratory in

Portland, OR, this database is geared toward providing both a reference and registry service for school districts, educational agencies, and other educational institutions. *RICE* provides users with access to information concerning the producers of educational software packages as well as descriptions of instructional and other software packages. *RICE* will contain 2,000 citations by 1983; it dates from 1979 to the present and is updated bimonthly with approximately 250 records. Citations not only contain marketing contact information and descriptive text, but detail systems requirements for software packages, and suitable hardware types. Independent evaluations of instructional packages are also frequently included. Descriptors are from the *Thesaurus of Eric Descriptors*. *RICE* is available to all users with no royalty charge at present.

PDQ: A New National Cancer Institute Database

A new database, PDQ (Protocol Data Query), became available on the NLM system October 1, 1982. *PDQ* was developed by the National Cancer Institute (NCI) so that information regarding current methods of cancer methods of cancer therapy in NCI-supported programs would be more widely accessible for the benefit of physicians and their patients. *PDQ* currently contains general descriptions (the protocol objective and the patient entry criteria) of approximately 700 cancer therapy research protocols. With each protocol, there is a list of institutions where the protocol is being used to treat patients and the name, address and telephone number of an oncologist to contact at each institution for information about the protocol. Monthly updates to this file are expected.

Protocols included in the present implementation of *PDQ* are those utilized in studies directly supported by the NCI and performed by the following groups: Cooperative Study Groups; Comprehensive Cancer Centers; Intramural NCI groups; and institutions under contract to NCI for Phase II and Phase III studies. It is anticipated that additional study groups will be added to the database in the near future. The *PDQ* file is closely related to the *CLINPROT* file.

Searchers receiving inquires on the *PDQ* database from patients or the public may refer these inquiries to Karen Schlick, National Cancer Institute (NCI), 800/638-6694 or 301/496-5583. Inquiries from health professionals or members of the media may be referred to the Database Manager, NCI, 301/496-7403.

Engineering Meetings Database Announced

SDC is now offering *EiMet,* the *Ei Engineering Meetings* database developed by Engineering Information, Inc. *EiMet* includes significant published proceedings of engineering and technical conferences, symposia, meetings, and colloquia from more than 40 countries. Over 2000 publications will be covered annually in all aspects of engineering and related disciplines: civil, environmental, geological, and biological engineering; electrical, electronic, and control engineering; chemical, agricultural, and food engineering; mining and fuel engineering; mechanical, automotive, nuclear, and aerospace engineering; and industrial and management applications.

The file covers July 1982 to date, and contains more than 32,000 records. Monthly updates add approximately 9500 records. *EiMet* serves as a companion file to *COMPENDEX* which cites entire conference proceedings but does not index individual conference papers. Connect hour rates for *EiMet* are $80 per hour; print costs are $.20 per citation online, and $.30 per offline print. All papers indexed in *EiMet* are available from the Engineering Societies Library via SDC's online ordering system.

BIOSIS Announces Zoological Record Online

The BioSciences Information Service (BIOSIS) has announced the availability of *Zoological Record Online,* the machine-readable version of the world oldest and largest index to the zoological literature. *Zoological Record,* published jointly by BIOSIS and the Zoological Society of London, has applications for research in all areas of zoology, such as animal behavior, genetics, physiology, evolution, communication, anatomy, and systematics. Articles are indexed from over 6000 serials; theses, monographs, conference proceedings; and special reports are also scanned. The indexing contains both controlled and natural language.

The database currently consists of approximately 60,000 records from 1978 *only,* corresponding to volume 115 of the print index. Bimonthly updates of more current data are planned for 1983. Costs for searching the database, available on DIALOG as File 185, are $78 per connect hour and $.20 per full record printed offline.

NLM MEDLINE Backfiles Online

The National Library of Medicine (NLM) has announced a major change: the availability of all its *MEDLINE* backfiles as online files, effective December 13, 1982. This change was made possible due to the increased storage capacity of NLM'S new IBM 3033 MP system. The files have been resegmented as follows:

1. *MEDLINE* will be a 3-year file growing to a 4-year file containing 1980-1983 material.
2. *MED 77* contains 1977-1979 data.
3. *MED 75* covers the 1975 and 1976 files.
4. *MED 71* covers the 1971-1974 material.
5. *MED 66* will cover the 5 years 1966-1970.

Offsearches for the files will continue to be available.

SEARCH SYSTEM NEWS

AMA/NET Offered

The American Medical Association and the GTE Telenet Medical Information Network have announced the availability of a network of information services which includes information bases and electronic mail. AMA/NET is one of several information networks currently being aimed at the health practitioner as end user. We will be describing additional networks in future issues.

MED/MAIL the electronic mail component is intended for use as a "universal communications system" available to all network members. It features information retention, group list, bulletin board, electronic forms, and document ordering capabilities.

Current information bases are: Drug Information; Disease Information; Medical Procedure Coding and Nomenclature; and Socio/Economic Bibliographic Information.

The Disease Information base, produced by the AMA Department of Medical Terminology and Nomenclature contains current, succinct descriptions of diseases, disorders and conditions. The important diagnostic features of more than 3500 identifiable diseases are summarized in a systematic manner, using preferred standard terminology. The disease base is organized in such a way that users can request information on a specific disease in its entirety or for certain subtopics under the disease listing.

The Drug Information base produced by AMA's Division of Drugs contains evaluative, up-to-date and unbiased information on the clinical use of drugs. More than 1500 individual drug preparations marketed under some 5000 trade names in the United States, Canada and Mexico are described in detail. Users will not only be able to obtain comprehensive information for each drug by name but will be able to identify drugs according to indications for therapy, special patient circumstances, or for certain drug actions and interactions. The database is an enhanced version of *AMA Drug Evaluations,* 5th edition, 1983. One-twelfth of the information base is routinely updated each month. Critical additions and revisions are made immediately.

The Medical Procedure Coding and Nomenclature information base, developed by the AMA Department of Medical Terminology and Nomenclature, is derived from the *Physicians' Current Procedural Terminology,* 4th edition, 1981, with semiannual updates. It provides a uniform coding and nomenclature system for reporting medical services and procedures performed by physicians. It contains more than 6000 descriptions of procedures with their identifying codes in the areas of medicine, surgery and diagnostic services.

The Socio/Economic Bibliographic Information base, produced by the AMA Division of Library and Archival Services, serves as a guide for locating current articles on the non-clinical aspects of health care. More than 700 journals are monitored on a continuing basis, making this the most comprehensive bibliographic resource of its kind. Other sources include legislative reports, books and selected newspapers. Subject areas covered include economics, education, ethics, international relations, legislation, medical practice, political science, psychology, public health, sociology and statistics. This file which has no current print counterpart should provide much improved subject access over its predecessor, the print index known as *Socioeconomic Research Sources* (MEDSOC). Plans are to update it monthly.

Start-up costs for AMA/NET vary. Usage charges are approximately $26 per connect hour.

BRS Increases System Hours

BRS is now available for searching 7 days a week, between the hours of 6:30 a.m. and 4 a.m. Eastern time.

SDC Announces Online Cost Display

SDC is now providing an online cost display. Options include an automatic cost feature, displays of session costs since login; file charges with each change of files, print costs for online and offline prints requested, and a detailed printout of all charges and total costs.

NLM Discontinues Use of SUNY Computer

With the installation of its new computer system in Semptember 1982, the National Library of Medicine no longer required the use of a backup computer at the State University of New York. All NLM users can now go directly to NLM for access to all its database.

BRS/After Dark for Home Computer Users

The BRS search system is now available to the personal computer user at a fraction of the standard business day charges. BRS/After Dark couples a user-friendly interface with the sophisticated BRS/SEARCH software. BRS/After Dark allows personal computer users access to many of the same comprehensive databases available in the daytime at drastically reduced rates during the after-business hours of 6 p.m. until midnight, local time. These files contain information from millions of journals, reports, books and articles and range over hundreds of fields including business, computers, medicine and others.

BRS/After Dark is easy-to-use and, because of its menu-driven design, requires no formal training. The service is available for a one-time subscription fee of $50 which includes the BRS/After Dark Newsletter and User Manual. Access to BRS/After Dark is available for a minimum fee of $6 per connect hour which includes UNINET telecommunications charges. There is a $12 per month minimum usage fee. Individual database royalties have been reduced for the BRS/After Dark program and are not included in the $6 per connect hour charge.

A Personal Note

Sci-Tech Online usually confines its reports to news about online databases and search systems of interest to the readers of this journal. We have not attempted to detail the arrival and departure of individuals involved in the sci-tech information scene. We would now like to make an exception to this policy. We cannot let the resignation of Jan Egeland as President of BRS go unnoticed in this space.

Jan's contributions to the development of online information retrieval are well-known. She oversaw the development of the SUNY BCN from its infancy to its utilization in major universities and medical schools. The innovative and flexible search features of that network were carried over to BRS, which she co-founded. Most important in both these ventures was Jan's insistence on user-oriented systems, fair pricing, user education, and quality assurance. Jan's presence at BRS will be missed by many; her influence will continue to be felt.

SCI-TECH IN REVIEW

Suzanne Fedunok, Editor

PERIODICAL ARTICLES

Library Standards

Stinson, E. Ray. Standards for health sciences libraries. *Library Trends.* 31(1): 125-137; 1982 Summer.

This article, written by the Resource Information Coordinator of the Office of Sponsored Academic Programs of the University of Texas Medical Branch at Galveston, discusses the histories and salient points of current standards used to define levels of performance in hospital libraries (the 1978 *Accreditation Manual for Hospitals* of the Joint Commission on the Accreditation of Hospitals) and in academic health sciences libraries (the 1979 guidelines of the Liaison Committee on Medical Education). The last section is devoted to a discussion of the MLA certification program for librarians, last revised in 1981.

The author concludes that the last decade has seen "major improvements" in the development and use of standards.

"Grey" Literature

Availability and bibliographic control of non-conventional literature. *Aslib Proceedings.* 34(11/12):507; 1982 November/December.

While dealing primarily with information sources in the United Kingdom, this issue of the *Proceedings,* which reports on a one-day Aslib conference held in London on May 24, 1982, should be of interest to American librarians as well. Speakers from national libraries, government, education, industry and the EEC read papers on "non-conventional" or "grey" literature, ie, that literature not issued through normal commercial publishing channels. Technical reports, theses, conference papers, trade literature, translations, are among the categories of materials in question, and since we share many of the same problems with these types of publications, the suggestions advanced here should be of common interest.

The papers read were: "Grey literature—the role of the British Library Lending Division," by David Wood (pp.459-465); "Market research reports, house journals and trade literature," by David King (pp. 465-472); "Local government information: a 'grey area,'" by Barry Nuttall (pp.473-479); "Grey literature online: the GLC experience," by Tim Owen (pp.480-486); "Commercial sources of non-conventional literature: the catalogue of the British Official Publications not published by the HMSO and Business and Government," by Charles Chadwyck-Healey (pp.487-492); "Grey literature worldwide: the UAP programme," by Stephen Vickers (pp. 498-505).

INSPEC Analysis

Hawkins, Donald J. INSPEC on Dialog. *Database.* 5(4):12-25; 1982 December.

This article, by the supervisor of the Information Retrieval and Alerting Service at Bell Laboratories in Murray Hill, NJ, will serve as an in-depth guide of how to use INSPEC on Dialog. INSPEC, which stands for International Information Services for the Physics and Engineering Communities, has, as the author points out, "an excellent reputation among librarians and information specialists in the scientific and technical areas" particularly in physics, electronics engineering, and computer science. The major topics covered by the author are the Subject coverage of the online products, the Search aids provided by INSPEC, and in admirable depth the Searchable fields. Sample searches are given in tables at the end, to illustrate his points on the special features on INSPEC, and the author concludes that its coverage is good and timely, but that the database lacks quality control, is difficult to search for chemical names, and is inconsistent in its controlled vocabulary.

Title Word Study

Diodato, Virgil. The occurence of title words in parts of research papers: variations among disciplines. *Journal of Documentation.* 38(3):192-206;1982 September.

In response to an earlier concern by Buxton and Meadows that "there may be gross differences between subjects in the usefulness of title words" as points of access in bibliographic retrieval, the author, whose PhD thesis is also described in this issue, reports on his research to answer the question "How well does the title of a paper in a given discipline reflect the content of the paper?"

The title words, abstracts, first paragraphs and last paragraphs, as well as cited titles of papers from five journals in chemistry, economics, history, mathematics and philosophy from the 1960s and 1970s were analyzed. Differences among these fields were noted which might have an effect on the kind and depth of indexing needed to design sensitive information retrieval systems for them. In general the author discovered that these types of journals resembled each other in the manner in which title words appeared in their articles and it seemed that the title words used reflected fairly accurately the content of the articles.

The author concludes that "there is more similarity than difference among chemistry, economics, history, mathematics and philosophy with respect to how well the titles of their articles indicate their article content and how the article parts reflect the occurence of words in their titles."

Survey on the Electronic Journal for Physicists

King, Donald W.; Roderer, Nancy K. Communications in physics—the use of journals. *Physics Today.* 35(10):43-47; 1982 October.

In a recent article Donald King and Nancy Roderer, president and vice-president of a consulting firm specializing in communications research reported on several studies done on the world of publishing as it affects physicists. They discuss the preferences of readers, how physicists obtain journal articles, what they are willing to pay for articles, the move toward "separates or preprints and offprints of journal articles, the impact of page charges, the impact of interlibrary loan, and much more information of interest. Perhaps one of the most significant findings of the article is the importance of the library to researchers in physics. "Physicists are unique among scientists in how they obtain their journal articles. They do a much lower proportion of their reading from personal subscriptions than do other scientists . . . . Currently, physicists use library copies of journals for nearly half of their article readings." Furthermore, what physicists are using are not the older articles in the library archives, but rather the most recent articles. As King and Roderer report:"Our surveys show that about 65% of the articles read by scientists and engineers are less than one year old, and about 85% are less than 3 years old."

The authors outline the reasons why they feel there is "a great deal of appeal" in the idea of distributing articles on demand, as with an online journal, but they conclude that scientists as users, publishers, authors, and libraries will all need important incentives to change before this is widely adopted.

DOCTORAL DISSERTATIONS FROM DISSERTATIONS ABSTRACTS INTERNATIONAL

Retrieval of Mathematics Documents

Diodato, Virgil Pasquale. *Author indexing in mathematics.* Urbana-Champaign, IL. University of Illinois; 1981. 238 p. Order no. 8127592 from University Microforms International, 300 N. Zeeb Rd., Ann Arbor, MI 48106.

Mr. Diodato's research was to test the *major* hypothesis that mathematician "authors would demonstrate better retrieval performance than professionals" (ie, than the mathematician editors of *Mathematical Reviews*). The study involved the comparison of the *AMS(MOS) Subject Classification Scheme* numbers assigned by authors to their own papers with the numbers assigned by *Mathematical Reviews* editors to the same papers. Often the classification assigned by authors is not the same. The results of the study of 159 documents failed to support the hypothesis; there was no significant difference to readers (mathematics faculty and graduate students at the Mathematics Department of the University of Illinois) in their ability to recall papers by the classification number assigned by the author versus that assigned by a *Mathematical Reviews* editor.

Readers were also asked to supply their own classification numbers for the documents in question, with the result that the reader-assigned classification numbers resulted in a slightly higher retrieval rate than that of the professional editors.

Finally, a test of the consistency among the various groups was performed, with the conclusion reached that "authors performed as well as professional indexers in this experiment, despite the assumed advantage of experience held by professionals." Perhaps the most interesting result of the research, however, was the failure of readers to recall half the documents in the major hypothesis test. Mr. Diodato attributes this in part to the unfamiliarity of the investigator/searcher with specific subject areas in mathematics (although they were graduate students and faculty members in a mathematics department), and to the failure of the AMS *Scheme* to have better systems of cross references, scope notes, hierarchical arrangement, and synonym control.

Can Citations Predict Important Literature?

Hurt, Charlie Deuel, III. *Identification of important literature in quantum mechanics: investigation of a bibliometric and an historical approach.* Madison, WI: University of Wisconsin; 1981. 288 pp. Order no. 8124612.

In this study four histories of quantum mechanics were examined and the references each author used to support his historical analysis were analyzed. The second means of selecting important literature was through frequency of citations of literature spanning the years prior to 1937. Statistical tests were run on the results gathered, and the results were as follows:

1. The association between the rankings of cited items using a citation analysis approach and the ranking of cited items using an approach which pools the references used by historians in their reconstructions of the period is statistically non-significant.

2. Association between the attributes chosen to investigate particular areas of potential difference in the two literature distributions is non-significant and supports the conclusion above.
3. The use of citation analysis alone or historical analysis alone will not result in the same set of literature being produced than would result if both methods were used. Using citation analysis to predict important literature in a scientific area appears to be risky since another method which would ostensively produce the same literature of importance did not.

Frequent corporate entries in sci-tech Literature

Tikku, Upinder Kumar, *Use of corporate entries for the literature of science and technology.* Pittsburgh: University of Pittsburgh; 1981. 197 pp. Order no. 8202337.

Using the OCLC catalog online to study the extent of use of corporate entries in the literature of science and engineering, to look for the justification of making such entries, to study the catalog system for finding solutions to problems through "unobtrusive measures," and to study whether or not the application of AACR 2 and CCC for corporate entries led to an empirical hyperbolic distribution, the author also used the *American Book Publishing Record Cumulative 1950-1977* and SPSS and other FORTRAN programs.

The conclusions were that there is a high frequency of use of corporate entries (13%); the use of corporate body entries seems to be justified; there is a hyperbolic distribution shown in the application of AACR 2 and Ranganathan's *Classified Catalog Code* and a "core" of rules for corporate main entry in both AACR 2 and CCC. Finally the author demonstrates that a mechanism exists for the theoretical prediction of the number of cataloging rules, given the number of entries, and vice versa.

Wide Use of Literature from the "For Profit" Sector

Koenig, Michael Edward Davison. *A bibliometric analysis of pharmaceutical research.* Philadelphia: Drexel University; 1982. 174 pp. Order no. DA8213393.

To quote from the author's summary: "Pharmco articles (U.S. based for-profit pharmaceutical companies) were found to be highly cited, particularly in the area of biomedical research, where they appear to be on a par with NIH funded medical school articles. This has implications for policy, as it indicates that pharmaceutical research may have some scientific outputs that are of far broader utility that just to the pharmaceutical company concerned, outputs that policy formers may wish to encourage."

TECHNICAL REPORTS

Recent NTIS Reports

Selander, Sally E.; Payne, Elizabeth A.; Freiberger, Gary; Brogan, Linda B. *The Integrated Library System (ILS):User manual.* McLean, VA: MITRE Corporation; 1981; PB 82-114968. 292p.

The Integrated Library System (ILS) is a minicomputer-based library automation system designed to support a full range of technical processing and retrieval activities using a single master bibliographic file (MBF). Current subsystems include: bibliographic control using MARC format records; catalog access online; circulation functions; serials control; and administrative functions such as the setting of processing parameters and display records. THE ILS is implemented under the MIIS/MUMPS operating system, which is available on DEC, Data General Eclipse, and IBM Series 1 microcomputers and may be obtained from Meditech, Inc. 255 Bent Street, Cambridge, MA 02141.

Subsequent releases of ILS are to include full serials control and acquisitions which is to be written in the MIIS/MUMPS programming language for implementation on a Data General Eclipse C/330 computer using Meditech MISS 4.5 operating system. 128K bytes of core storage are required to operate the system. The source tapes and software are available (contact NTIS/Computer Products for price quote) under the following numbers: Goldstein, Charles M. and Robert Borochoff. *Integrated Library System (ILS)* Bethesda, MD: National Library of Medicine; 1981; PB 82-114950; Mag tape NLM/DF-81/003. Supporting documentation has appeared under numbers PB80-202674; PB80-202666; PB81-128340; PB81-128357; PB82-114968 and PB81-188039.

Future of Scientific and Technical Communication

Clayton, Audrey. *The potential influence of social, economic, regulatory and technological factors on scientific and technological communication through 2000 A.D.* Volume One: *The forecast.* Arlington, VA: Forecasting International Ltd.; 1981; PB 82-129917. See also Volume Two (PB 82-129925).

Volume One of this report, done by Forecasting International Ltd. under an NSF grant, treats the weighty subject of the future of scientific and technical communication by studying the impact of "potentially disturbing factors" in case studies of bibliographic retrieval services. The point of view is that of the user of scientific and technical information, and the report identifies key policy issues as well as trends and their implications for decision-makers in government and industry.

BOOKS

World Guide to Bibliographic Services

The General Information Program of UNESCO in Paris has since 1951-52 been compiling annual reviews of bibliographical services throughout the world and issuing cumulations every five or ten years. The latest cumulation was prepared by Mlle. M. Beaudiquez of the Bibliotheque Nationale in Paris and covers the period 1975-1979. Both this cumulation and the latest annual volume (1980) were due to appear in 1982 and may be obtained from Division of the General Information Program, UNESCO, 7 Place du Fontenoy, 75007 Paris FRANCE. Requests for this material should be addressed to the attention of Mme. C. Coudert-Schklowski, who is also engaged in a review of the format, frequency and utility of these publications to their users. In that regard, Mme. Coudert-Schklowki invites the users and contributors to this publication to contact her office in writing with comments and suggestions.

LETTER TO THE EDITOR

Dear Sir:

I wish to call your attention to some inaccuracies in the State Union Lists given by Tucker and Cerutti [V.2,No.4]. While I am no authority, I do know that the union lists for the Pacific Northwest are not listed in their current editions and formats.

Oregon Regional Union List of Serials is updated bi-annually by the Oregon State Library. The 4th edition is scheduled for publication in late October 1982 and includes holdings for 135 libraries. It is available only in microfiche. A new Serials Titles is published in intervening years.

The *Directory of Serials in Washington State Libraries* is no longer published. Instead the *Washington Library Network Resource Directory* is a union list of monographs, serials and audiovicuals. Updates are published annually in early January and it is available in microfiche.

Not listed by the authors was the *California Union List of Periodicals* now in the 7th edition (1982). It includes holdings for over 450 libraries. It is available on BRS as well as in microfiche. This is certainly to be considered a more valuable resource than the *Oregon Regional Union Lists of Serials*.

Marcia Buser-Molatore
Technical Information Specialist
Precision Castports Corporation
Portland, OR

EDITOR'S NOTE: The authors reply that they relied on current entries in the LC catalog. They feel this letter points out one of the many problems in finding union lists.

For Product Safety Concerns and Information please contact our EU representative GPSR@taylorandfrancis.com
Taylor & Francis Verlag GmbH, Kaufingerstraße 24, 80331 München, Germany

www.ingramcontent.com/pod-product-compliance
Lightning Source LLC
Chambersburg PA
CBHW052134300426
44116CB00010B/1896